THE
FLYING INSTRUCTOR'S
PATTER MANUAL

THE
FLYING INSTRUCTOR'S
PATTER MANUAL

A word for word account of all
the flying exercises
as spoken in the air

Peter Phillips & Robert Cole
Illustrated by L. R. Williams

ADVANCED SECTION

INCLUDES
AIRCRAFT ASSESSMENT

Airlife
England

Airlife Publishing Ltd

101 Longden Road, Shrewsbury SY3 9EB, England

Contents

3

ACKNOWLEDGEMENTS

To Squadron Leader Tim Carter for his incisive advice, to Sue Phillips for her assiduous typing and to The Oxford University Press for permission to quote from Fowler's "Modern English Usage".

Foreword by
Air Commodore D. Allison

Commandant, Central Flying School, Royal Air Force

Flying, as with most activities that take place in the elements, is challenging and great fun. But aircraft can be very unforgiving of careless errors, therefore, flying is a sport that must be approached with due respect. Many years ago the Royal Air Force learned the hard way that the only proper foundation for a flying career is expert instruction by a trained, qualified and enthusiastic flying instructor. This Flying Instructor's Patter Manual is a labour of love by two experienced and able ex-Royal Air Force flying instructors. Rightly, the authors do not offer patter for each lesson to be followed verbatim, but they do provide a carefully thought through presentation for most essential exercises from which the inexperienced instructor can develop his own patter and from which the experienced can refer to refresh their memories. However, the underlying reason behind the book, which I strongly support, is the duty laid upon the flying instructor to take his student into the air with himself fully briefed and rehearsed on the exercise to be flown. This duty falls upon the instructor for two reasons. First, because the student is buying his services and has a right to expect value for his money, and, secondly, because it is incumbent upon all flying instructors to ensure that they spare no effort to drive home the fundamentals of flying so that their protégées may enjoy safely the tremendous exhilaration of flying with a sound understanding of the limits and skills involved. For all the above reasons I recommend this reference book to those engaged in the enjoyable but demanding profession of flying instruction.

January 1983

Introduction

We had been reminiscing on how difficult it had been to form one's own 'patter' when we first started instructing; how we had tried to memorise the best phrases and words used by our course instructors, and regretted that it had not been possible to take notes. We also remembered later on, when we were relatively experienced, how it had been almost as difficult to re-apply ourselves to an exercise that had not been practised for a long time. We both agreed that it would have been an absolute godsend, many times over, to have been able to refer to a verbatim account of 'patter'. Upon that day this book was born.

We believe that 'off-the cuff', 'play it as it comes', type of flying largely belongs to a bygone era. Although the modern fighter pilot still has to retain flexibility, even he now refers to a manual which tells him the best manoeuvres to employ in a dogfight against a particular foe. In another field, a Shakespearean actor would never dream of making up his own dialogue just because he knew the story of the play. We believe that, within reason, this also applies to 'patter'; there is a bad and a good way of doing it.

From the onset we were concerned with standardisation. We therefore, independently, wrote our own 'patter' for every exercise, and then compared notes. Much to our surprise we were largely in agreement. Even so, we criticised each other ruthlessly, timed areas where flying and 'patter' co-ordination were critical, and finally proved every exercise in the air.

We learned a lot ourselves, as sloppy 'patter' sometimes gets overlooked when delivered in the air, whilst in cold print it has to stand up to detailed scrutiny. We found stalling by far the most difficult exercise, and because it is so important, we spent much time fine-honing it.

'Patter' can never be done entirely 'by numbers'; there must be some flexibility and we do not think for one moment that it should be wholly stylised, for individuality, within reason, is the essence of progress. However, we do believe this manual must be fairly standard because it is based on the 'patter' used by hundreds of fine instructors with whom we have had the privilege of flying and to whom we dedicate this book.

Preface

An analysis of 'patter' reveals that it falls into four categories:

1. A combined commentary and explanation which is the most usual and normal format.
2. A very pithy and abbreviated commentary, used in such exercises as the stall recovery and aerobatics.
3. The short explanation.
4. Fault analysis.

To be effective, the normal format should include visual cues and some reference to control techniques. It is of little benefit, for example, to chant monotonously "Speed good, glidepath good", or, "Don't chase the airspeed", without telling the student how it should be done.

Another discrepancy that is seldom highlighted but is much more common than realised, is the instructor who uses a control technique during demonstrations which he does not actually teach. Dare we say that we have heard some very good instructors who 'patter' that they are controlling the speed with elevators but are, in actual fact, using the power. Pity the poor, confused student who sadly says to his friends, "My instructor has magic in his fingertips, I don't know how he does it".

One of the authors can well remember, in his early days of flying, being so confused by the then current method of teaching straight and level, that he said to himself, "Flying is not for me". When he dared to take issue with "Sir", whom he noted used a more logical technique, he was told not to argue, and to "shut-up".

The second category of 'patter,' the very abbreviated commentary, is used in demonstrations where it is difficult to harmonise 'patter' with the flying. Better to say simply "Opposite rudder and stick forward" for the spin recovery than to try to include the full procedure with all its nuances and in the process get hopelessly out of phase with the flying. In practice these phases of flight are nearly always preceded or succeeded by an explanation.

We spent much time considering and testing these critical phases of 'patter'. Even if some people disagree with the contents, we can at least guarantee that they can be co-ordinated with flying. In fact, it is sometimes difficult to reconcile realistic 'patter' with correct grammar. Fowler's "Modern English Usage" does provide a let-out. "It is well, on the other hand, not to give up what one feels is idiomatic in favour of an alternative, that is more obviously defensible". Occasionally we use the 'dash' to camouflage "indefensible" grammar, where there appears to be no alternative, but mostly to indicate a natural pause or control movement.

Both authors have benefited from the short, in-flight, explanation. It can jog the memory of the briefing and, if the topic is important, an emphatic explanation can make an everlasting impression. For those who do not approve, it should be mentioned that none of the 'in-flight' explanations in the text lasts more than 35 seconds.

Finally there is fault analysis. The secret is to analyse one's own technique precisely, as this will enable one more easily to spot control irregularities in others. Apart from verbatim 'patter', detailed control analysis is the raison d'etre of this book.

Negative teaching or demonstrations by default are not approved by some establishments. In a sense the recovery from the vertical is negative and we believe that there are other phases of flight which benefit from so-called negative teaching. Two examples are the incorrect use of the VSI and speed control during the climb.

The advanced section may upset some traditional instructors, for the piloting world is very conservative, perhaps because experience is more revered than in other professions. Nevertheless, we know of many fine aviators who use the techniques described, without perhaps knowing it or having analysed it themselves. However, it is not our intention to upset the status quo of traditional teaching and basic techniques. On the other hand, we do believe that by the time pilots have gained their PPLs they should have been made aware that there are alternative methods of flying which, in more critical conditions, can be more accurate, and, perhaps, easier and therefore safer.

For example, many experienced pilots have always used a form of Fixed Point navigation which has only in recent years been formalised by the Royal Air Force, who many consider to be the world's foremost exponents of high-speed low-level pilot navigation.

The ILS, described in the advanced section of this book, was first positively evolved by one of the authors, fifteen years ago. It was then considered to be heresy, but we now know that it is used as a standard technique in at least one school. We do, incidently, appreciate that there are other methods, equally as good, which might suit the individual better.

In recent years pure handling technique seems to have taken second place to systems management. Yet it is mishandling that causes most accidents. Unlike driving a car, it is quite difficult to arrange handling practice in an aeroplane. We believe that aerobatics are a marvellous way of developing orientation, feel and attitude for flying. In addition, the control technique used for station keeping in formation can, in many ways, be read across to flying the approach to land. Both are highly concentrated exercises, and it is interesting to note that at least one professional school was asked by airline management to include formation in their syllabus.

There are two exercises which we should like to discuss briefly in more detail. The first is stalling. Report after report tells of experienced pilots unaccountably stalling into the ground. It almost seems that the characteristic of the standard stall in level flight bears little resemblance to what actually happens in an emergency close to the ground. We do not wish to go into all the whys and wherefores, other than to mention one aspect. We believe that nose position relative to the horizon, is of vital importance for the recovery with most general aviation aircraft. The validity of this technique has been confirmed by observing very experienced test pilots flying new aircraft for the first time. Military jets do not necessarily come into this category as they can 'blast themselves out with power', although at high level they may find themselves in the same predicament. It is also worth mentioning that we believe that one period of low speed aerobatics (at height) can probably do as much good as 'months' of conventional stalls.

The second exercise we wish to discuss briefly is the final approach to land. It takes approximately 2 seconds, under ideal conditions, to look at the airspeed indicator and re-focus outside again. Checking the airspeed, therefore, below the screen or threshold height (approximately 50' AGL on a 3° glidepath) will never improve the situation. One should therefore, aim to stabilise the speed a good 4 seconds in advance, or with most general aviation aircraft at least 120 yards before the threshold. It is, in fact, quite a difficult process, and we therefore believe that a constant speed approach is more practical in the early stages of flying, in which emphasis is placed on an accurate glidepath, as well as speed.

As we point out in the practical I/F exercise, pitch changes with speed are extremely small at moderate angles of attack (applicable to most general aviation aircraft on the approach), when the glide or flight path is constant. If the latter is critical and the speed decays, such as during a wind shear, the lead control must be the throttle, although, if applicable, the nose-up pitch change must also be checked. In contrast, leading with the elevators will almost certainly result in an undershoot. In our view all pilots should be made aware of this before gaining their PPL. The advanced STOL exercise demonstrates how this is done.

At the end of the Preface is found the specification of the single and twin PR trainers, on which the visual references and performance of the text is based. To avoid complication we have kept the mnemonic check drills to a minimum, and for this reason the LIFE check is used with considerable flexibility.

It was only after studying 'patter' in depth, that we fully appreciated our own shortcomings. We are now convinced that effective 'patter', whatever the style, cannot be naturally acquired by the average pilot; it has to be learned.

Since the first edition the UK PPL syllabus has been amended to include slow flight as part of the stalling exercise, Exercise 10. Also spinning is no a longer mandatory exercise but nevertheless remains an essential exercise for the complete pilot.

Specification

P.R. SINGLE

GENERAL DESCRIPTION

The aircraft is a conventional side-by-side two-seat trainer with a low wing, a clear canopy and a tricycle undercarriage. It is equipped with a typical modern flat 4 aircooled engine with a fixed-pitch propeller and a carburettor heat control. It has three stages of flap; 10°, half and full. It is fully aerobatic.

Performance Parameters

General

Max. speed (level flight)	2700 RPM — 130 KIAS
Cruise speed	2300 RPM — 100 KIAS
Flap limiting speed	100 KIAS
Climb speed (clean)	Best rate 80 KIAS
Climb speed (10°)	Best rate 80 KIAS
Climb speed (half flap)	Best rate 75 KIAS
Climb speed (half flap)	Best angle 71 KIAS
Climb speed (full flap)	Best rate 70 KIAS
Stall speed (clean)	56 KIAS
Stall speed (half flap)	49 KIAS
Stall speed (full flap)	46 KIAS
V_{ne}	180 KIAS

Circuit

Base leg	80 KIAS
Final approach (powered)	75 KIAS
Final approach (glide)	80 KIAS
Threshold speed (short field)	60 KIAS
Rotation speed (clean)	65 KIAS
Rotation speed (take-off flap)	60 KIAS
Rotation speed (half flap)	55 KIAS

Specification

P.R. TWIN

GENERAL DESCRIPTION

The aircraft is a conventional side-by-side light twin. It is equipped with a retractable tricycle undercarriage, constant speed propellers, adjustable cooling gills, and two stages of flaps.

Performance Parameters

General

Max. speed (level flight)	165 KIAS
Cruise speed (2300 RPM — 23″ MP)	150 KIAS
Undercarriage limiting speed	140 KIAS
Flap limiting speed	130 KIAS
Climb speed (clean)	100 KIAS
Climb speed (take-off flap)	95 KIAS
Climb speed (full flap)	90 KIAS
Climb speed (single engine)	95 KIAS
Stall (clean)	74 KIAS
Stall (take-off flap)	68 KIAS
Stall (full flap)	64 KIAS
V_{mca} (left engine windmilling — take-off flap)	74 KIAS

Circuit

Safety speed (take-off flap)	82 KIAS
Safety speed (clean)	88 KIAS
Threshold speed	83 KIAS
Normal approach speed	90 KIAS
Rotation speed (take-off flap)	74 KIAS
Base leg	95 KIAS

Exercises 1a, 1b, 2 and 3 which cover aircraft familiarisation, emergencies, preparation for flight and initial air experience do not involve 'patter' as such and are therefore not covered in this manual.

EXERCISE 4 — EFFECT OF CONTROLS — PART I

NOTE: (1) Refer to Turning for adverse yaw
demonstrations.

Aircraft Position in Flight Profile

The student and instructor are in the cockpit prior to starting the pre-flight checks.

Air Exercise

"Are you comfortable now you have strapped in?"

STUDENT ANSWERS

"Make sure you adjust the seat so you can reach and operate the flying and engine controls easily. Once you have found a seat position that suits you, use it on all flights.

First let's cover following through on the controls and then the procedure for handover and takeover of control. Look how I place my feet on the rudder pedals, heels on the floor, one hand on the control column and the other on the throttle. This is how you will hold the controls when you are flying the aircraft.

When demonstrating exercises, I will sometimes ask you to follow me through. Now, as you would in the air, take hold of the controls lightly; lightly so you can follow but not interfere with the control movements. Feel the movements I make — elevator up, elevator down — left aileron, right aileron — now, relax.

In the briefing I explained how we hand over and take over control. When I say to you, 'You have control', you put your hands and feet lightly but positively on the controls, and then say, 'I have control'.

Conversely, when I wish to regain control for a new demonstration I will say, 'I have control'. You relinquish control and acknowledge by saying, 'You have control'.

Let us have a dry run.

You have control."

STUDENT ANSWERS. "I HAVE CONTROL."

INSTRUCTOR. "I have control."

STUDENT ANSWERS. "YOU HAVE CONTROL."

"Good, it is essential that the hand over and take over of control is positive and if you are ever unsure who has control, don't hesitate to ask."

Aircraft Position in Flight Profile

Aircraft in the climb away from the airfield. The instructor has control.

Air Exercise

"Are you comfortable and can you hear me clearly?"

STUDENT ANSWERS

"In the air we must discipline ourselves to keep a good lookout. Remember any aircraft that stays on a constant bearing is a collision risk. Look from left to right, scanning up and down as you do so. If you see another aircraft point it out, interrupt if necessary. A good lookout must be practised, so that it is as natural as breathing."

Aircraft Position in Flight Profile

Aircraft in level flight at 2500'. The instructor has control.

Air Exercise

"The aircraft is now in the normal cruise attitude, at 2500', and 100 Kts. The attitude of the aircraft can be judged by relating the position of the nose and the wing tips to the earth's horizon. You can see that, with this aircraft, the nose is about 6″ below the horizon and that the wing tips are equidistant below the horizon. Also note that the coaming is parallel with the horizon. We'll use this cruise attitude and speed as a reference, to look at the effect of the controls on the aircraft.

Follow me through. Try to remember this position of the control column, it's neutral. First we'll look at the elevators. They are controlled by fore and aft movement of the control column. Watch the horizon. Pulling the control column back smoothly, you can see the nose moving up above the horizon. The movement continues until I return the control column to the neutral position. Now the nose is above the horizon and the speed has decreased.

Conversely, easing the control column forward, again smoothly, the nose moves down in relation to the horizon and continues to go down until I return the control column to the neutral position. The nose is below the horizon, we are in a nose down attitude and the speed has increased to 120 Kts. Finally, ease the control column back to raise the nose to the initial cruise attitude.

We call this motion 'pitching'. You can see how the elevators control the aircraft's nose attitude and how smoothly the controls were moved. I would like you to try the elevators; you will notice a change of stick force with speed; we will cover this later on. You have control."

STUDENT PRACTISES.

"I have control. Now let us have a look at the ailerons. Follow me through. The ailerons are controlled by turning the control column left or right. Here we are in the cruise attitude. Note the position of the nose and wing tips relative to the horizon. Turning the control column to the left, the left wing is going down and the right wing is coming up. We're rolling to the left. Centralise the control column and the roll stops. We are now banked to the left.

To roll the wings level with the horizon, smoothly turn the control column to the right. The left wing is coming up and the coaming is nearly parallel with the horizon. Centralise the controls and the roll stops.

Turning the control column to the right, the right wing goes down and the left wing comes up; we're rolling to the right. Centralise the ailerons, we stop rolling and we're banked to the right. Finally roll back to wings level with left aileron.

I would like you to try the ailerons, roll both left and right. Is that clear?"

STUDENT ANSWERS

"You have control."

STUDENT PRACTISES.

"I have control. Good. Now let us see how the rudder affects the aircraft Follow me through on the rudder pedals. Pick a feature ahead on the horizon as a reference; that cloud will do.

Pushing the left pedal, you can see the nose moving round the horizon to the left; we call this motion 'yawing'. Centralise the rudder pedals and, although the nose returns a little to the right, we have, in the main, moved well to the left of the reference point.

Similarly pushing on the right rudder pedal, the nose yaws to the right until the rudder is centralised. I want you to yaw the aircraft left and right when I give you control of the rudder pedals. Tell me how you find the pedal forces compare with those of the control column. In the next exercise you will see how we use the rudder pedals to balance the aircraft in flight. You have control."

STUDENT PRACTISES AND ANSWERS.

"I have control. Yes, they are high compared with the control column forces.

So far I have emphasised that we use the controls smoothly with comparatively small deflections. We will now have a look

20

at the aircraft's response to larger control deflections. In the briefing I explained that this is most easily seen in the rolling plane. Follow me through. Watch the horizon and tell me what you think of the roll rate — applying a small aileron deflection."

STUDENT ANSWERS

"Yes, it is low, now increasing the aileron deflection, you can see a faster roll rate. The response to elevator and rudder is also related to control deflection, but is less easy to see. I want you to try the ailerons to confirm what I have just demonstrated. You have control."

STUDENT PRACTISES.

"I have control. Let us have a look at the effect of controls in a different attitude. Follow me through. Putting the aircraft into a banked attitude to the left, tell me which way the nose moves when I apply the controls. Easing back on the control column, what's happening?"

STUDENT ANSWERS

"Yes, the nose moves up in relation to us. Apply left rudder and you can see the nose yaws to the left, again in relation to the aircraft's axis. Clearly the controls work relative to the aircraft's axis and not the earth's horizon. Try that yourself. You have control."

STUDENT PRACTISES.

"I have control. Here we are back in the cruise attitude. We will now investigate the further effect of the controls. In the briefing I explained that the elevator has no further effect. So let us look at the ailerons. Follow me through. Put your feet firmly on the rudder pedals and watch the attitude. Rolling the aircraft to the left, you can see the nose is now yawing left and is going below the horizon. We're entering what is known as a spiral dive to the left. To recover, roll the wings level and raise the nose into the cruise attitude. The primary effect of aileron is roll and the secondary effect is yaw; this resulted in a spiral dive. I want you to try that yourself but use right aileron. You have control."

STUDENT PRACTISES.

"I have control. What happened when we applied rudder?"

STUDENT ANSWERS

"Yes, the aircraft yawed either left or right. In the cruise attitude again with my hands off the control column, put your feet on the rudder pedals. Follow me through. Watch the nose. Applying left rudder, we yaw to the left and almost straight away roll to the left. Adding a little more rudder, you can see further yaw and roll and finally we enter a spiral dive. Centralise the rudder and we recover to the cruise attitude, using aileron and elevator. Repeat that yourself but use right rudder. You have control."

STUDENT PRACTISES.

"I have control. So far our speed has been about 100 Kts. Let us have a look at the effect of airspeed on the feel and response of the controls. I will leave the throttle in this position, at 2300 RPM. Increasing the speed to 120 Kts. by lowering the nose, I want you to try each control in turn to assess the response and how they feel; try to remember the results. You have control."

STUDENT PRACTISES.

"I have control. You could see that the controls became firmer and more responsive with increasing speed. Now decreasing the speed to 75 Kts. by raising the nose, I want you to make similar control inputs and compare them with those at 120 Kts. You have control."

STUDENT PRACTISES.

"I have control. You can see that, at a low speed, to produce any appreciable change in attitude we require quite large control deflections. The controls are also not so responsive and do not feel so firm, but nevertheless they still work satisfactorily.

We will now have a look at the effect of slipstream on the controls. Follow me through. Closing the throttle to reduce the slipstream, and holding 80 Kts., I want you to make aileron, elevator and rudder inputs and remember the results. You have control."

STUDENT PRACTISES.

"I have control. Now increasing to full power and holding 80 Kts., make the same control inputs and compare them with the last results. You have control."

STUDENT PRACTISES.

"I have control. What do you think?"

STUDENT ANSWERS

"Yes, the ailerons remain the same but the rudder and elevator are more responsive because of the increase in the slipstream.

Now let us consider the use of the elevator trim. Setting 2300 RPM and returning the aircraft into the cruise attitude, when I give you control, tell me if you have to push or pull on the control column to hold the aircraft steady. You have control."

STUDENT PRACTISES AND ANSWERS.

"I have control. Yes, you have to push. If you had to hold this load for any length of time it would be very tiring.

I will now show you how to remove the load with the trimmer. Holding the exact attitude with the elevators, wind the trim wheel forward until the push force is zero. Use coarse movements to begin with and when the force is lighter, move the trim wheel more slowly. I am now relaxing my grip on the control column to feel the slightest pressure through my fingertips, so that I can remove the last trace of load. Now releasing the control column, you can see the aircraft maintains its attitude. Remember what I said in the briefing; if you are pushing on the control, wind the trim wheel forward; if you are pulling, wind it back. It works in the natural sense.

When I give you control I want you to hold the attitude absolutely steady, whilst I move the trim wheel. You have control."

STUDENT PRACTISES.

"Winding the trimmer now, are you pulling or pushing and which way do you have to turn the trim wheel to remove the load?"

STUDENT ANSWERS

24

"Now feel for the trim wheel, don't look for it, and trim out the loads. You have control."

STUDENT PRACTISES.

"Remember to hold the attitude steady with the control column, as you trim; this is most important. Tell me when you have removed all the loads."

STUDENT ANSWERS

"Now, release the control column to see how the aircraft maintains its attitude. Fine, that is good. You obviously trimmed precisely and the aircraft's natural stability did the rest.

I have control. Accurate trimming is an art and the hallmark of a good pilot, but don't use it to adjust the attitude. You will see the importance of accurate trimming in the next exercise."

END OF EXERCISE.

EXERCISE 4 — EFFECT OF CONTROLS — PART II

Aircraft Position in Flight Profile

Aircraft in the cruise attitude at 3000'. The student has revised Effect of Controls Part I, including trimming.

Air Exercise

"I have control. We'll start today's exercise by looking at the effect of airspeed on engine RPM. The engine power is controlled by the throttle; this setting gives us 2300 RPM at 100 Kts. Lowering the nose with elevator to increase the speed, look, the RPM has gone up to 2400 RPM at 120 Kts. Conversely, raising the nose to slow down you can see the RPM reducing as the speed decreases, although I have not touched the throttle. Remember then that the RPM will change with speed at a fixed throttle setting.

Now let's have a look at the effect of power changes on the trim of the aircraft. Here we are in the cruise attitude, with 2300 RPM, and hands and feet off the controls. Tell me what happens when I decrease power. Watch the nose — throttling back to idle."

STUDENT ANSWERS

"Yes, the nose moved to the right and down. To stop that happening and to hold the attitude steady, you must use a little left rudder and up elevator.

Again setting 2300 RPM in the cruise attitude, this time I will increase to full power. Watch the nose. Power going on, you can see the nose moves up and to the left. Normally, we stop this happening with down elevator and right rudder.

I will now show you how to co-ordinate the use of rudder and elevator to prevent the nose moving when the power is altered. Follow me through and feel the control movements as I change the power.

Once again in the cruise attitude, increase the power and simultaneously apply right rudder and forward pressure on the control column to hold the nose steady. Now reducing the power, progressively apply left rudder and back pressure on the control column to maintain the nose position. Have you any questions?"

STUDENT ANSWERS

"I want you to practise increasing and decreasing power whilst maintaining the attitude precisely. It is most important that you do this accurately and instinctively as you will see later on. You have control."

STUDENT PRACTISES.

"I have control. It helps to remember that with engines that rotate in a clockwise direction, the yaw is to the left when you increase power, and to the right when you decrease power; this applies to most American engines.

Now let us have a look at the effect of flap. Remember the briefing; flap gives extra lift and drag at a given airspeed. This is useful, especially for landing. The white arc on the ASI goes up to 100 Kts. and shows the flap limiting speed. The flap is controlled by this lever and has four positions, up, 10°, half and fully down. We will ignore the 10° position as it has no significant effect with this aircraft; its main use is to increase elevator authority during take-off. The half position, however, increases the lift considerably, but only adds a relatively small amount of drag. Flap fully down on the other hand, produces a lot of drag, but only a small further increase in lift.

Notice we are trimmed, hands and feet off at 85 Kts. Watch the nose and tell me what happens when I select half flap — lowering half flap now."

STUDENT ANSWERS

"Yes, the nose pitches up. Therefore to regain our original attitude, I have to apply a forward pressure on the control column like this; feel it for yourself whilst you hold the attitude. You have control."

STUDENT PRACTISES.

"I have control. Also look at the speed, it has decreased because of the extra drag.

Once again trimmed in the cruise attitude with hands and feet off the controls, watch the nose and the speed as I lower full flap. Flap going down, the nose comes up very slightly, but the speed is decreasing rapidly.

I will now raise the flap in stages. Trimming the attitude for 65 Kts., and releasing the controls, watch the nose as I select flap up to the half position — the nose goes down only slightly but the speed increases. Retrimming with hands and feet off the controls, watch the nose again as I raise the flap fully up — the nose immediately goes down; and to regain this attitude I have to ease back on the stick. Did you feel the sink?"

STUDENT ANSWERS

"Now hold the back elevator to feel the pull force. You have control."

STUDENT PRACTISES.

"I have control. The reason for the sink is the sudden loss of lift. This and the change of trim is why we raise the flap in stages and observe the height and speed limits, in particular in the circuit.

I have retrimmed the aircraft and I want you to hold this attitude as you lower and raise the flaps in stages. Retrim between each stage. Remember with this aircraft, when you lower flap the nose comes up and when you raise it the nose goes down. Try to check the movement. You have control."

STUDENT PRACTISES.

"I have control. To complete the exercise I will cover the use of the carburettor heat and the mixture control. First the carburettor heat, this knob here. Note the RPM is 2300. Pulling the carb. air out into the hot position, the RPM drops 150 revs. Returning it to the cold position, the original RPM is restored. In principle, exercise it once every 10 minutes for about 10 seconds, as carburettor icing is insidious. I will tell you more about this on the ground. However there is a danger of detonation if you apply it at full power for any length of time.

The mixture is controlled with this knob here. Don't confuse it with the carburettor heat because if you pull it right out to idle cut off, the engine will stop. Fully in, it is maximum rich. Watch the RPM as I slowly pull it out. There, you can just see the revs. initially increase but have now dropped slightly, and the engine is running roughly. Pushing it in, approximately $\frac{1}{8}''$, to regain smooth running, this is the optimum lean position. I will tell you more about it later, but remember, in principle, never lean above 75% power.

That is the end of the effect of controls. It is an important exercise to understand, if you wish to fly well. Have you any questions?"

STUDENT ANSWERS

"Good, I will fly you back to Springfield but you can direct me.

END OF EXERCISE.

EXERCISE 5 — TAXYING — NOSEWHEEL TRICYCLE UNDERCARRIAGE AIRCRAFT

Aircraft Position in Flight Profile

The aircraft is being taxied by the instructor well clear of the parking area.

Air Exercise

"You can see how I hold the control column central, my left hand on the throttle and feet on the rudder pedals. It is important to keep your heels on the floor, as it possible to inadvertently apply brake when pushing on the rudder pedal to operate the nosewheel steering. Follow me through.

Pick a point well ahead and you can feel I am pushing the left pedal forward and we turn to the left; similarly pressing the right pedal and we turn to the right. In other words we can steer on the ground simply by using the rudder as it is connected to the nosewheel steering. I will give you control of the rudder pedals and you can practise steering the aircraft. I will ask you to make some turns. You have control."

STUDENT PRACTISES.

"I have control. As well as steering the aircraft we must control its speed; we do this by throttle and toe-brake. Look at the left wing tip and you can see how fast we are moving; this is the correct speed.

If I increase power a little, like this, you can see we are moving faster. Conversely throttling back to idle and we are slowing down. On level ground such as this we normally need just a little power to maintain our speed. However, when the ground is very hard or on a concrete surface, idle power is sufficient to keep the aircraft moving.

To slow and stop the aircraft, first close the throttle and then use the toe-brakes. Looking ahead to keep straight, bring the power to idle and smoothly press the toe-brakes evenly to stop in a straight line; use the nosewheel steering if necessary. Taxying forward again, I want you to practise stopping. You have control."

STUDENT PRACTISES.

"I have control. When we are stationary it is normal to apply the parking brake. To do this press the toe-brakes in, pull out the catch and release the brakes. If the parking catch stays out it shows that the brakes are on. Finally reset the power to 1200 RPM to prevent the plugs oiling up. To move off, first bring the throttle to idle, now release the parking brake by pressing on the toe-brakes and make sure that the catch goes in. Checking that we are clear ahead and on both sides, increase power to about 1500 RPM until we start to move. Now test the brakes like this. Close the throttle and smoothly apply the toe-brakes to slow the aircraft — they are obviously working. Release them, open the power as before and the aircraft accelerates forward again. When it is travelling about this speed, reduce the power to just above idle to maintain our progress.

I want you to stop the aircraft and practise moving off. Remember never use brake against power; it is unnecessary and wears out the pads. You have control."

STUDENT PRACTISES.

"I have control. Normally one holds the elevator neutral and sets the aileron into wind. You can see we have a crosswind from the right at 2 o'clock. To prevent the wing lifting I am putting on right aileron. If the wind had been from the right and behind, I would have put on left aileron. Also be aware of the tendency for the rate of turn to increase when taxying downwind, although this is not normally a problem with a tricycle undercarriage.

When moving from one surface to another do so one wheel at a time. If you cross at right angles you might easily find that the main wheels will get wedged if the surface levels are uneven. Like driving a car up on to a pavement, approach slowly, at an angle, one wheel at a time.

Finally you often find yourself having to taxy in confined spaces. The watchword is 'caution'; stop if in doubt and never trust marshallers implicitly. Follow me through. Look out to the left, it is clear. I will turn through 180°, using the nosewheel steering. Note the radius of turn and the speed with which the right or outer wing travels. Also remember to check that your tail is clear of obstacles. Lastly consider what is behind you. There may be an open hangar or another aircraft, so do not use excessive power. Now you try some minimum radius turns. You have control."

STUDENT PRACTISES.

END OF EXERCISE

EXERCISE 5 — TAXYING (TAILWHEEL AIRCRAFT)

Aircraft Position in Flight Profile

The aircraft is in dispersal, with the pre-starting checks complete.

Air Exercise

With a tailwheel aircraft, you must take more account of the surface wind than with a tricycle undercarriage aircraft. For starting, the aircraft should be normally positioned into wind like this. As you crank the engine, keep the stick well back. I want you to start up and then I will show you taxying. You have control."

STUDENT PRACTISES.

"I have control. First make certain that all is clear in front, now release the brakes and only apply minimum power to move forward, as harsh use of brake can tip the aircraft on its nose. Now close the throttle and test the brakes gently. Moving forward again, you can see the view in front is obscured by the nose, so swing it from side to side, like this, to clear the area

33

ahead. It is a bit tedious sometimes, but never relax as taxying accidents with tailwheel aircraft are legion.

As we are taxying downwind, do it slowly and keep braking to a minimum. If the wind is high or greater than the slipstream effect on the tail, consider holding the stick forward. Today we will just play it as the demand requires; you can sometimes feel the residual force on the elevator. Also remember that if you turn whilst taxying downwind, the wind can sometimes accelerate the turn. Now continue to taxy towards the take-off point. The wind is not very high, so keep the stick well back in your stomach, and remember to weave the nose. You have control."

STUDENT PRACTISES.

END OF EXERCISE

EXERCISE 6 — STRAIGHT AND LEVEL — PART I

Aircraft Position in Flight Profile

Aircraft climbing away from the field. The instructor has control.

Air Exercise

"Can you hear me clearly?"

STUDENT ANSWERS

"In the briefing I stressed the importance of lookout. I explained how we use the clock-code to report other aircraft or features on the ground relative to us. We take the left wing tip as the 9 o'clock position, the nose as 12 o'clock and the right wingtip as 3 o'clock. The tail is obviously 6 o'clock. For example, look to the left of the nose, there is a long village. I would report it as a "village left, 10 o'clock, range 4 miles." If it was an aircraft, you would also report it as "level, high or low," relative to us. In addition you might say which way it is going, such as "moving left to right". How would you report that wood just behind the left wing tip?"

STUDENT ANSWERS

"Good, now levelling off in the cruise attitude, when I give you control hold the attitude and trim the aircraft. After that I will upset the trim a few times so you can practise further re-trimming. You have control."

STUDENT PRACTISES.

"I have control. This, in fact, is the cruise attitude for straight and level flight. We determine our attitude by relating it to the earth's horizon. You can see where the earth and the sky meet in a saucerlike line. Look at the wing tips and you can see they are equidistant below the horizon. From a more practical point of view, note where the nose and coaming are relative to the horizon.

We can confirm that we are straight and level on the flight instruments. The altimeter is steady at 3000', the DI indicates 270° and finally the slip ball is central. Also we have 2300 RPM set, which gives us 100 Kts., our cruising speed.

We will start with level flight, and how to maintain it. This is the attitude for level flight at 100 Kts., with the nose about 6" below the horizon for this aircraft. The altimeter shows we are steady at 3000'. Follow me through.

Raising the nose above the horizon like this, you can see we are no longer level because the altimeter reading is increasing. To regain level flight, lower the nose with the elevator to the original attitude and hold it. Retrim, if necessary, and finally check to see if the altimeter is steady; it is.

This time lowering the nose, you can see the attitude is wrong, and as a result the altimeter is showing a loss of height. To regain level flight, raise the nose to the original attitude, hold it and check the altimeter; it is still showing a slight descent. We must therefore raise the nose a fraction more like this, and hold it. Referring to the altimeter again, it is steady, confirming we are in level flight. Now trim the attitude exactly.

Remember, make all attitude adjustments by relating the nose to the horizon; we only glance at the altimeter to check whether the attitude is correct.

I will now disturb the aircraft in pitch, initially without altering the trim and I want you to return it to level flight. You have control."

STUDENT PRACTISES.

"I have control. Fine, we have been flying for some time and must guard against becoming too engrossed in the exercise to the detriment of safety and good airmanship. I will complete a LIFE check but, from now onwards, I will expect you to do it yourself. Obviously I will help you in the early exercises. L is for location and lookout. Where are we, in this case in relation to Springfield? You can see the disused airfield at 3 o'clock; this means we are about 6 miles West of base. As regards lookout, keep it going, scanning up and down through the horizon from wing tip to wing tip. I is for instruments. Check the vacuum pressure is in the green. With the wings level at a steady speed compare the compass with the DI. If necessary synchronise it like this. I will explain this in more detail later. F is for fuel. Check you have sufficient to complete the exercise safely. Change to the fuller tank if they are out of balance by more than one quarter; put on the pump as you do it and monitor the fuel pressure. E is for engine. Check all the instruments are in the green sector and exercise the carburettor heat for a few seconds; note the RPM drop and its value when the control is pushed in; more about this later. Also you can see I have leaned the mixture; I will explain this more fully to you on the ground.

We will continue the exercise by looking at straight flight. You can see that we are flying directly towards that large cumulus cloud, which we will use as our reference point. In other words we are maintaining straight flight, confirmed by the DI which is steady on 280°. To achieve this, we use the ailerons to keep the wings level with the horizon, and the ball in the centre,with the rudder; I will come to that later. Follow me through. Watch the nose and the horizon. Lowering the left wing you can see the nose deviating to the left from our reference point. To regain it, apply a small amount of right bank with aileron like this, and the nose returns to the reference point.

Now roll the wings level, which we can verify by looking from the left wing tip through the nose to the right wing tip. In other words we use the ailerons to maintain straight flight.

I will now displace the aircraft from wings level a few times and would like you to correct back to straight flight using a suitable reference point. Is that clear?"

STUDENT ANSWERS

"You have control."

STUDENT PRACTISES.

"I have control. Will you please carry out a further LIFE check."

STUDENT PRACTISES.

"Good, now we will consider balanced flight. You can see we are still at 3000', at 100 Kts. with the slip-ball central. Notice we are heading towards the corner of that wood on the hill at 12 o'clock.

Follow me through. Applying left rudder and sufficient opposite bank with aileron to maintain our heading, you should feel that you are slipping towards my seat. Note the slip-ball position, it is hard over to the right. Yet a check outside shows we are still holding a constant direction towards the wood, although the nose is pointing slightly to its left. Note the controls. The rudder is to the left, and the ailerons are to the right. We are flying with crossed controls, which, as you will find later, can be dangerous at low speeds. It is also inefficient because, if you look inside, you will see that the speed is 10 Kts. slower than when the ball was central at the same power setting.

Levelling the wings with aileron, but keeping on left rudder, you can now see the nose yawing round the horizon to the left. The ball is still out to the right and we are in a skidding turn; this is not, however, the way to do it. Correcting the yaw with right rudder and the movement is stopped, but a check of the slip-ball shows it to be half-a-width out to the right; we must still be flying with crossed controls without knowing it.

The slight out-of-balance can only be seen by referring to the slip-ball and it should therefore be monitored and corrected constantly during most phases of flight. If the ball is out to the right like this, apply right rudder until it is in the centre and hold it. Conversely, if it is out to the left like this, apply left rudder. The correction is in the natural sense, but remember, in principle, you never maintain direction with rudder, but instead keep the aircraft balanced, with the ball in the centre.

Putting the aircraft into unbalanced but straight flight like this, I want you to centralise the ball with the rudder but at the same time maintain direction with the ailerons. You have control."

STUDENT PRACTISES.

"I have control. We will now look at a typical disturbance in which we have to make a correction on to a given height and heading. Here we are straight and level at 3000', on a heading of 270°. I will disturb the aircraft slightly. Follow me through.

You can see we are nose high and banked to the right. To correct, roll the wings level with aileron and smoothly lower the nose to the correct attitude. Visually check for any obvious yaw, and confirm on the slip-ball. The attitude looks correct, but a check on the instruments shows we are slightly high at 3050', and have deviated right onto 290°. To regain the heading, apply 10° of left bank like this — 270° coming up so roll the wings level. To regain 3000', ease the nose down about 3″ on the horizon and momentarily hold it there — 3000' coming up so raise the nose to the level attitude, hold it and retrim. Finally check inside again and you can see the altimeter and DI are steady and the slip-ball is central. If they were not, we would have to make minor corrections as before.

I will displace the aircraft slightly and when I give you control return to 270° and 3000'. You have control."

STUDENT PRACTISES.

"I have control. To conclude the exercise I want to cover the normal sequence you should adopt in flying straight and level. Combine the lookout with an attitude check. Start searching from left wing tip, looking up and down, through the nose to check the attitude. Then look inside to confirm all is correct on the altimeter, DI and slip-ball. After this continue the lookout round to the right wing tip. When you have completed this sweep, look up above, over the top of the canopy and back to the left wing tip to start again.

Finally remember, because of its inherent stability, if the aircraft is disturbed from its flight path it will tend to return to it, provided it is correctly trimmed. I will show you.

Here we are precisely trimmed for straight and level flight. Raising the nose slightly with elevator and now releasing the control column, look — the nose slowly returns to the horizon, goes through it slightly and after a few diminishing cycles regains level flight. If it did not have this stability, it would be very difficult for you to write in the log or read a map. However the aircraft has to be correctly trimmed and the controls held lightly. Have you any questions?"

STUDENT ANSWERS

"Good, you can now fly the aircraft back to the airfield. You have control."

STUDENT PRACTISES.

END OF EXERCISE.

EXERCISE 6 — STRAIGHT AND LEVEL — PART II

NOTE: (1) Note that pitch attitude changes with speed are very small in level flight compared to the normal climb and the glide, which can be three times as great. This is not often appreciated.

Aircraft Position in Flight Profile

Aircraft in straight and level flight at cruising speed. Student has completed a short revision of straight and level, at a constant power setting. The instructor has control.

Air Exercise

"We will start this exercise by looking at the effect of power on straight and level flight, or, in other words, how we increase and decrease speed.

You can see we are in the familiar cruise attitude for 100 Kts., and I want you to particularly note the nose position for this aircraft; as I see it, it is about 6″ below the horizon.

Follow me through. Remember the effect of power will cause a nose-up pitch change unless prevented, so, holding this attitude exactly and the wings level with aileron, smoothly increase to full power and correct the yaw with rudder. You can now see the speed is increasing and, if you watch the altimeter, you can see we are just starting to climb. To correct this, I must lower the nose a little, and to remove the 'push' force, I will trim forward. Holding this new attitude, look at the altimeter; we are starting to climb again. I can anticipate this by progessively lowering the nose as the speed increases, removing any stick force with trim. Judge the rate of lowering the nose by monitoring the altimeter.

The speed has now stabilised at 130 Kts., and you can see that the RPM has also increased up to the red line, 2700. This is the maximum speed for this aircraft in level flight. Note the nose position, it is about 2″ lower than at the cruise. This is the lowest pitch attitude for this aircraft in level flight with the flaps up. Remember it.

41

Looking inside, the DI, altimeter and slip-ball confirm that we are straight and level, in balanced flight.

The technique then, to fly faster in level flight, is to lower the nose progressively as the speed increases, although the attitude changes are relatively small. Don't forget to trim, and keep the aircraft balanced.

Throttling back and returning to the cruise attitude, I now want you to repeat that acceleration, and hold the aircraft steady at 3000'. Monitor the altimeter but don't become mesmerised by it. You have control."

STUDENT PRACTISES.

"I have control. We will now have a look at the effect of reducing power. Again, I will initially hold the attitude constant, so we can see what happens. Remember that decreasing power causes a nose-down pitch, so I must prevent this with back pressure.

Follow me through. Watch the speed. Reducing power to 2000 RPM, balance with left rudder and hold the nose attitude with back elevator. Immediately, we start to slow down. Check the altimeter and you can see we are descending, so to stop this, I must progressively raise the nose as the speed decreases, simultaneously trimming out the pull force. Coming through our cruise speed, note the familiar nose attitude, but continue to raise the nose as the speed decreases. Retrimming, the aircraft has now stabilised at 75 Kts. with a higher nose attitude; it is just above the horizon. Remember it. This is the lowest speed and the highest pitch attitude that this aircraft will normally operate in level flight.

Inside, the DI and altimeter are steady and the ball is central. Also note, even though I set 2000 RPM at 130 Kts., it has now reduced to 1700 RPM without moving the throttle.

When I give you control, first set full power and stabilise at maximum level speed, and then repeat what I have just done. Occasionally check the altimeter, but most of the time you should look outside, making small but progressive attitude changes. You have control."

STUDENT PRACTISES.

"I have control. Good, before we go on to the next part of the exercise, carry out a LIFE check, please."

STUDENT PRACTISES.

"We will now apply our knowledge of attitude changes, in order to select particular speeds in level flight. Let's first start by making small increases in speed. I will go from 75 to 80 Kts. and, as a rough guide, this will require an increase of about 50 RPM.

Follow me through. Increasing to 1750 RPM, I still maintain straight and level flight by fractionally lowering the nose as the speed slowly increases. It has now stabilised at 82 Kts., and to achieve the precise figure, reduce the power a note or two, and there we are at 80 Kts. Now trim as finely as possible, and check for balance.

Using the same technique, I want you to increase the speed to 85 Kts. You have control."

STUDENT PRACTISES.

"I have control. Clearly, it would be a slow process using the same procedure for large speed increases, say 15 Kts., or above. I will now increase speed to 100 Kts., using a slightly different technique.

Follow me through. This time, opening to full power, check the yaw and nose-up trim, and as the aircraft accelerates, smoothly and progressively lower the nose to maintain level flight, at the same time trimming out the loads. As we pass 95 Kts., anticipate, slightly, for 100 Kts. and select 2300 RPM., the approximate power setting. Once the aircraft has stabilised, make small adjustments, as before, to achieve the precise speed. We are very slightly slow, so I will increase power a fraction and trim the attitude exactly. I hope you can now see how useful it is to know the correct attitude for every speed. This is the secret of straight and level flight.

I now want you to increase speed to 115 Kts., using a rule-of-thumb of 50 RPM per 5 Kts. The power required will, therefore, be approximately 2450 RPM, but first open to full throttle. You have control."

STUDENT PRACTISES.

"I have control. To slow down, we reverse the process. First, I will demonstrate a small reduction in speed, but as we find the aircraft slows down more easily, we can take a small change up to 20 Kts. Let us select 100 Kts.

Follow me through. Allowing for speed effect, set 2350 RPM and as we decelerate, hold level flight by progressively raising the nose, keeping the wings level and the ball in the centre. Wait for the aircraft to stabilise and trim. 102 Kts., so a fraction back on the power to precisely achieve 100 Kts. Finally, trim and check the slip-ball is central.

I now want you to carry out a similar deceleration down to 90 Kts,. and then to re-accelerate up to maximum speed. Hold the aircraft level throughout. You have control."

STUDENT PRACTISES.

"I have control. Fine, for larger speed reductions, we can. hasten the process by closing the throttle fully. I will slow down to 100 Kts. from 130.

Follow me through. Closing the throttle fully, check the yaw, and as the speed decreases, raise the nose smoothly to hold the height. Anticipating 100 Kts., select 2300 RPM, and as before, make small power adjustments to achieve 100 Kts. precisely.

I now want you to accelerate to 110 Kts., and then slow down to 80 Kts., at the same time maintain straight and level flight. Remember to trim, keep the ball in the centre and try to anticipate height deviations by progressively adjusting the nose attitude. Once again, don't become mesmerised by the altimeter. Have you any questions?"

STUDENT ANSWERS

"You have control."

STUDENT PRACTISES.

"I have control. To complete the exercise, let's compare straight and level flight with flap up and down.

Follow me through. Selecting 80 Kts. with 1750 RPM, you can see the nose is quite high. Watch the nose move in response to the control movements — aileron — rudder — elevator. Not very crisp at all. Mainly, though, note the nose attitude.

You can see we are well below the flap limiting speed, marked on the ASI by the white arc, so lowering half flap, stop the speed decreasing by opening the throttle to 2200 RPM, and to hold level flight, I have lowered the nose about 4″ on the horizon. Checking inside, the altimeter, DI, slip-ball and ASI confirm that we are in straight and level flight at 80 Kts. For the same speed, therefore, half flap needs more power and a lower nose attitude to maintain a constant height; as a result we have a better view forward.

Also, let us check the control response as before — aileron — rudder — elevator; the rudder and elevator feel firmer due to the increased slipstream but the aileron response has not changed.

Now lowering full flap, I must open the throttle almost to full power to maintain 80 Kts. But, look, I hardly need to change the nose attitude to hold the height. There is little merit in flying like this in level flight, but it does show the large increase in drag with full flap.

Always raise the flap in stages to avoid excessive trim changes. Holding the present attitude, raise the drag flap to half and throttle back to hold the speed. Retrim. Now lifting half flap, I must raise the nose to maintain level flight, and to hold the speed must throttle back to 1750 RPM. Finally retrim and check the ball for balance.

Now you practise lowering and raising the flap in stages, at the same time holding a constant height and speed. You have control."

STUDENT PRACTISES.

END OF EXERCISE.

EXERCISE 6 — STRAIGHT AND LEVEL — FLYING ON THE WRONG SIDE OF THE POWER CURVE

Aircraft Position in Flight Profile

Normal cruise at 3000'.

Air Exercise

"In the briefing, I told you that the speed requiring minimum power for this aircraft in level flight was 70 Kts. First set 1500 RPM to allow the aircraft to slow down. Now, just as 70 Kts. approaches, select 1650 RPM and use the power to bracket the speed if necessary, but 1650 RPM seems good.

Theoretically, this is the endurance speed, but practically, we add on 5 Kts. to allow for turbulence and control inputs.

To fly on the wrong side of the power curve, first select 1500 RPM to slow down for about 3 seconds, simultaneously raising the nose to hold the height. Now, increase the power to 1750 RPM and, look, the speed has stabilised at 63 Kts; the speed is lower and yet the power is higher.

Now, rather than alter the power, we will put the aircraft into a gentle descent, like this. You can see the speed is increasing towards 80 Kts. Easing out of the dive into level flight and adjusting for 1750 RPM, you can see we are now holding 80 Kts. at the same power setting as for 63 Kts. I think this adequately demonstrates that with this aircraft you can fly at two speeds for one power setting.

I want you to try this for yourself. Hold this height and reduce power to about 1500 RPM until the speed is 63 Kts. Then set 1750 RPM and repeat the last part of the demonstration. You may have noticed that the pitch changes with speed are more pronounced at these high angles of attack. It requires fairly fine flying, so hold the stick lightly. You have control."

STUDENT PRACTISES.

END OF EXERCISE.

EXERCISE 7 — CLIMBING

Aircraft Position in Flight Profile

The aircraft is in level flight, having just departed the circuit.

Air Exercise

"I will now demonstrate how to climb. Follow me through. Before entering the climb we must carry out a thorough lookout. Search from the left through the nose and above the aircraft, to the right and to the rear, to make sure it's clear.

Checking that the mixture is rich and the carb. air is cold, open up to full power and simultaneously raise the nose to this attitude. Apply sufficient right rudder to check the yaw and keep the wings level with aileron. Now hold this attitude steady and trim out the elevator force. This is the climbing attitude;

remember it. I will now level off and give you control, so you can practise entering a climb. Any questions?"

STUDENT ANSWERS

"You have control."

STUDENT PRACTISES.

49

"I have control. Follow me through. Now let us see how to level off. It is clear, so smoothly lower the nose to the level attitude, like this. Allow the speed to increase to 100 Kts., and at the same time continue to lower the nose to hold the height; simultaneously, trim out the forward pressure on the stick. 100 Kts., coming up, so power back to 2300 RPM, check the yaw and, finally, make small adjustments for the exact height and speed. Retrim precisely. Checking inside, the DI and altimeter are steady, the ball is central and we are holding 100 Kts.

I now want you to enter a further climb and practise levelling off. Then put the aircraft into another climb, so we can cover how to maintain it. You have control."

STUDENT PRACTISES.

"I have control. For the initial practise, we have accepted a basic attitude for the climb, but we should aim to hold 80 Kts. exactly, as this gives our best rate of climb. Look, the speed is 83 Kts., 3 Kts. too high, so, to correct, raise the nose slightly to a new attitude, hold it and trim. Make a positive pitch attitude change. You must wait for the speed to settle down after you adjust the attitude, unless it goes below 80 Kts. in which case readjust to a lower nose attitude. Be patient, guard against the tendency to chase or follow the airspeed. Finally check the ball is central; it can have quite an effect on the rate of climb, especially at higher altitudes.

As well as maintaining the correct airspeed, we must also monitor the temperatures and pressures every 1000' or so. Remember the engine is working at full power, at a relatively low airspeed; temperatures can become critical in hot countries. Also, note that the VSI is indicating 700 feet per minute up; we will check this later on in the climb.

Don't, however, get hypnotised by cockpit indications. Lookout during the climb is just as important as in other phases of flight. There are two ways of clearing the area hidden by the nose.

We can weave the nose from side-to-side, in this case by lowering the right wing, like this, using about 10° of bank, so that we can check the area to the right and especially below. Now, reversing the bank, we can clear the area to the left, originally hidden by the nose. Finally, roll the wings level and resume the climb.

Alternatively, if we want to hold our heading, gently lower the nose like this, and clear the area ahead and below. Then smoothly re-enter the climb.

When I give you control, I want you to level off. Then enter a further climb and hold it. Also, carry out a lookout as I have demonstrated. After that, I will take control and we can cover levelling off at a given altitude. Don't forget the engine checks. You have control."

STUDENT PRACTISES.

"I have control. Look, the rate of climb has decreased to 600 feet per minute. As I explained in the briefing, it will decrease with increasing altitude. To level off at 4500', we anticipate by one tenth of the rate of climb, in this case 60'. 4440' coming up, so smoothly lower the nose to hold level flight, occasionally monitoring the altimeter and adjusting the attitude as the speed increases. Trim out the loads. 100 Kts. approaching, so throttle back to 2300 RPM, check the yaw and make small adjustments to power and attitude, to hold 4500' and 100 Kts. exactly. Finally retrim precisely, and recheck the slip-ball. Have you any questions?"

STUDENT ANSWERS

"I now want you to enter a further climb and then level off at 6000'. In the briefing, I explained that we reduce the climb speed by 5 Kts. at 5000', to 75 Kts; this is to preserve the best rate-of-climb. You have control."

STUDENT PRACTISES.

END OF EXERCISE.

51

EXERCISE 7 — CLIMBING WITH FLAP

NOTE: (1) It is assumed, that with this aircraft, there is little sink or trim change whilst raising full flap to the half position, and, therefore, the speed at this stage is not increased in advance.

Aircraft Position in Flight Profile

Aircraft is straight and level at 1000′ AGL at 90 Kts. The instructor has control.

Air Exercise

To complete the exercise, let us have a look at climbing with flap down. This mainly applies to circuit flying. Follow me through.

Checking the speed is below 100 Kts., lower full flap and re-trim. I will add some power to stop the speed decreasing too much. First the lookout, from left to right and above; it seems all clear. Now, applying full power with rudder to balance, raise the nose into this attitude for 70 Kts.; this is the full flap climbing speed. Retrim and, look, the nose is much lower than in a normal climb.

Also, you can see we are barely climbing. In fact, there is no point in continuing like this; we must raise the flap. We do this in two stages to avoid sink and large trim changes.

Immediately raise the flap to half, hold the attitude and let the speed increase to 75 Kts., the best rate of climb with half flap. To maintain the speed, raise the nose slightly, hold it and trim. You can see a higher nose attitude than before and a more

respectable rate of climb, around 400' per minute. Notice there was little trim change or sink with this stage, but a large decrease in drag.

Finally, we can raise the half flap. Checking that we are at least 200' AGL, first increase the speed to 80 Kts. and now raise the flap smoothly, simultaneously easing the nose up into the normal climb attitude to hold 80 Kts. Retrim. You can see the rate of climb has increased to 700' per minute.

Notice that, before raising half or lift flap, I was careful to increase the speed to 80 Kts.; at low level, also check that you are at least 200' AGL. Sink at this stage can be quite pronounced, especially for a heavily laden aircraft.

I now want you to level off, lower full flap, and enter a similar climb. Then, as I demonstrated, raise the flap in two stages, calling out the limitations as you do it. You have control."

STUDENT PRACTISES.

END OF EXERCISE.

EXERCISE 8 — DESCENDING — PART I

Aircraft Position in Flight Profile

Aircraft in level flight at cruising speed.

Air Exercise

"Remember in the briefing, I said that we normally carry out certain checks before descending, as you are often letting down to join the circuit at this stage of your training. We therefore check that we have set the altimeter sub-scale to the airfield QNH, put the fuel pump on and set the mixture rich. Also, before entering the glide, we must clear the area beneath the nose and wings.

Follow me through. Looking to the left, turn to search the area beneath us. It seems clear, so roll the wings level, select carb. air hot, close the throttle, check the yaw with left rudder, and maintain the height until the speed is just above 80 Kts., the glide speed. Keeping the wings level, now lower the nose to the glide attitude, like this, hold it and trim. Note the attitude. I

will level off. First, I want you to clear the area, and then put the aircraft into the gliding attitude. Any questions?"

STUDENT ANSWERS

"You have control."

STUDENT PRACTISES.

"I have control. Good, now let's have a look at levelling off. Follow me through. Look, the rate of descent is 700 feet per minute. I will level off at 3000′ and will anticipate this by about 100′.

3100′ coming up, so carb. air cold, and setting 2300 RPM, simultaneously raise the nose into the level attitude. Check the balance and monitor the altimeter for final pitch adjustments. Retrim. Looking inside, the DI, altimeter, slip-ball and ASI should confirm we are in straight and level flight at 100 knots. If not, make small corrections with the power, attitude and rudder. Have you any questions?"

STUDENT ANSWERS

"Right, I would like you to enter a glide and then level off. After that, put the aircraft into a further glide and I will show you how to maintain it. You have control."

STUDENT PRACTISES.

"I have control. Here we are stabilised in the glide. Remember in the briefing, I said that we normally glide for maximum range, which requires a precise speed. For this aircraft we use 80 Kts. Follow me through.

Look at the speed, it is 84 Kts. — too fast. To correct, raise the nose slightly to a new attitude, hold it and trim. Wait for the speed to settle, then check again — yes — it's 80 Kts.

Similarly, if we are slow, the nose attitude would be too high, like this. Again correcting, lower the nose a little, hold it and retrim. After it has settled, check the speed and adjust again if necessary. Remember, always make positive pitch attitude changes; never chase the speed.

Also in the glide, we must not neglect our lookout. To do this, we periodically weave the nose to clear the blind spot, like this. Later on, during the circuit rejoin, you will see I use a continuous turn to clear the area below, as we can expect more aircraft there.

In a long glide the engine will cool rapidly, so we must open it up every 1000' to keep it warm. This is how it is done.

First select carb. air cold, and now smoothly open to full throttle, raise the nose to hold the speed, check the yaw and count for 2 seconds — one-thousand-and-one, one-thousand-and-two — now, throttle to idle, balance and re-establish the glide. Finally, carb. air hot and retrim.

I want you to continue with the glide, holding precisely 80 Kts., and then practise a lookout weave and finally warm the engine. After that, I will give you a height to level off. You have control."

STUDENT PRACTISES.

END OF EXERCISE.

EXERCISE 8 — DESCENDING — PART II

Aircraft Position in Flight Profile

The student has revised the 80 Kt. glide and levelling off. He has put the aircraft into a further 80 Kt. glide, and the instructor has taken control.

Air Exercise

"Here we are established in a glide at 80 Kts. with a rate of descent of 700 ft/min. We are gliding for maximum range.

Now if I lower the nose, hold this attitude and retrim. We are steady at 100 Kts. and look the rate of descent has increased to 1100 ft/min. So if we descend at a higher speed we lose more height.

Easing the nose up and back to a normal glide at 80 Kts.

I want you to try that for yourself and then return the aircraft to a normal 80 Kt. glide. You have control."

STUDENT PRACTISES.

"I will now show you the effect of power on the glide at a constant airspeed. Note the attitude and the rate of descent of 700' per minute. Follow me through.

Increasing the power to 1500 RPM, hold the attitude and look, already the speed is increasing towards 85 Kts. To regain 80 Kts., raise the nose slightly, hold it and retrim. Look at the rate of descent, it has decreased to 400' per minute. Increasing the power to 1700 RPM, we once again raise the nose to hold 80 Kts. The rate of descent is now only 200' per minute, and it is obvious that if we apply much more power we will level off or even enter a climb.

Now, reducing power to 1500 RPM, to stop the speed decreasing, I must lower the nose slightly, hold it and retrim. Once again the rate of descent is 400' per minute, and we are still holding 80 Kts. Throttling back further to 1200 RPM and lowering the nose, the rate of descent has now increased to 500' per minute. Finally, reducing the power to idle, lower the nose to hold 80 Kts.; we are, once again, back in the glide attitude. I will level off.

Lesson learned, in principle, we control rate of descent with

57

power and speed with the elevators. As a rough guide for this aircraft with flap up, a 200′ per minute change of descent, requires about 100 RPM change in power, and to hold a constant airspeed, the pitch has to be adjusted approximately 1″.

I now want you to practise varying the rate of descent with power and at the same time hold 80 Kts. with the elevators. Remember to make positive pitch attitude changes to adjust the speed. Start off from the glide with the throttle at idle. Have you any questions?"

STUDENT ANSWERS

"You have control."

STUDENT PRACTISES.

"I have control. We will now have a look at the effect of flap on the glide. Here we are once again at 80 Kts. with a rate of descent of 700′ per minute. I will hold the attitude constant and, checking that we are within the flap limiting speed, lower half flap, like this. Feel the lift, and look, the rate of descent has decreased a little, but the speed has reduced to nearly 70 Kts. To regain 80 Kts., lower the nose with elevators, hold it here, trim and now check the speed is steady again at 80 Kts. Note the lower nose attitude and the rate of descent which has increased to 1100′ per minute; in other words, when flap is lowered the rate of descent increases at a constant airspeed.

I will now lower full flap, but this time I will anticipate the effect in order to hold the speed. Selecting full flap, nose down to here, hold it and retrim. We have stabilised at 80 Kts., but look at the attitude, it is much lower and the rate of descent has increased to 1800′ per minute.

I will now level off without using power. Easing the nose into the level attitude, notice how quickly the speed 'washes off'; I must reapply power immediately to regain 80 Kts. Bear this in mind for future exercises, especially during glide approach

landings. In principle, never retract the flaps when descending close to the ground.

I now want you to enter a further glide and then hold 80 Kts. while you practise lowering the flap in two stages. Try to remember the different attitudes with flap to maintain the speed. This is a very common procedure, especially in the circuit. You have control."

STUDENT PRACTISES.

Aircraft Position in Flight Profile

Aircraft in the circuit on long finals at 1500′ QFE.

Air Exercise

"In the briefing, I said that the descending exercise is important because it leads up to control of the aircraft on the final approach.

Here we are lined up with the runway, with half flap and 1300 RPM set; a typical powered approach situation. Selecting full flap, I am having to lower the nose to hold the speed. Watch the end of the runway and tell me if it moves up or down the windscreen."

STUDENT ANSWERS

"Yes, it's moving up, so we would not reach the end of the runway if we continued on this flightpath; we are going down too fast. Increasing the power to 1500 RPM and raising the nose to hold 75 knots, let's now see what happens to the end of the runway. It's staying steady on the windscreen, which means we would reach the end of the runway; in fact this would be a good approach. Remember it. Adding a little more power and raising the nose to hold the speed steady at 75 Kts., look, the end of the runway is moving down the windscreen. We've now gone above the ideal glidepath; we are too high. To regain the glidepath, I must take off some power, like this, and simultaneously lower the nose to hold the speed. Tell me when you think we are on the correct approach path again."

STUDENT ANSWERS

"Good. To hold it I must reduce the rate of descent slightly by adding a little power and raising the nose to maintain 75 Kts. In fact, you cannot really separate the power and the elevator as nicely as that; one should co-ordinate their use.

I will demonstrate an overshoot. Coming up to 100', overshooting now, open to full power, rudder to balance and simultaneously raise the nose to hold 70 Kts. in a shallow climb. Confirming that we are above 100', raise the drag flap and trim for 75 Kts. Now, above 200', increase the speed to 80 Kts., and lift the remaining flap. To hold this speed, raise the nose slightly, retrim and continue the climb.

I will now position the aircraft on long finals again at 1500'. I want you to repeat what I have just done. Have you any questions?"

STUDENT ANSWERS

"You have control."

STUDENT PRACTISES.

END OF EXERCISE.

EXERCISE NUMBER 8 — DESCENDING — SIDESLIPPING

NOTE: (1) Sideslipping is a worthwhile exercise as the technique and co-ordination required are very similar to that of crosswind landings, especially the wing-down method.

Aircraft Position in Flight Profile

Aircraft in the practise forced landing area, at 3000', in a steady glide at 80 Kts. The instructor has control.

Air Exercise

"Here we are in a steady glide at 80 Kts. with a 700' per minute rate of descent. We can increase the rate of descent by sideslipping. However, a word of caution, sideslipping involves flying with crossed controls, so do not overdo it and also watch that the speed does not decay. Follow me through.

Do you see that large ploughed field ahead?"

STUDENT ANSWERS

"We will use it to maintain our heading. To sideslip to the left, apply some right rudder like this, and sufficient opposite aileron to keep us tracking towards the field. I must also lower the nose a little to maintain 80 Kts. Notice the nose is to the right of our field and we are banking slightly to the left.

61

Also, you may feel that we are slipping to the left. Look at the rate of descent, it has increased to over 1000′ per minute. If I now apply more right rudder, like this, I must also increase the bank to hold the heading. The rate of descent has increased even more, but, to hold the speed, I have lowered the nose.

To recover, smoothly remove the aileron and rudder together, level the wings and raise the nose slightly to stop the speed increasing.

I want you to practise a sideslip to the left, but remember what I said about excessive control deflections, and watch the speed. You have control."

STUDENT PRACTISES.

"I have control. I will now show you the slipping turn and then a sideslip as we might use them on the final stages of an approach. We will use that field at 11 o'clock to simulate a glide approach. Follow me through.

Here we are in the familiar 1000′ key position. Let us assume that we have limited flap and only wish to use it when we are certain of getting in. Commencing a turn to the left, it is obvious that we are too high. To increase the rate of descent, apply right, or top rudder like this, and hold the bank constant with aileron. Notice the nose is lower to maintain 80 Kts., but to hold it we have to apply back elevator. We are still high but we must come out of the turn. Continuing to hold right rudder, smoothly roll out of the turn but maintain the direction towards the field with the use of aileron; as before in the sideslip, the nose is offset. It is obvious we can now make it, so simultaneously centralise the rudder and ailerons, apply full flap and complete the final approach.

Overshooting now, carb. heat in and full power, I want you to climb to the 1000′ area and then practise a slipping turn and sideslip as I have just demonstrated. Is that clear?"

STUDENT ANSWERS

"You have control."

STUDENT PRACTISES.

END OF EXERCISE.

EXERCISE 9 — MEDIUM TURNS

Aircraft Position in Flight Profile

Aircraft in straight and level flight at cruising speed, 100 Kts. The instructor has control.

Air Exercise

"Before I demonstrate the entry into the turn, I want to show you the lookout, the attitude in the turn and to let you feel the back pressure required to stay level. Follow me through.

You can see we are in balanced flight, in trim at 100 Kts. at 3000'. We will turn to the left. First the lookout. We must search as far round to the left as possible, then sweep our eyes through the aircraft nose to the right, as this area will be blanketed by the wing in the turn.

Finally, look through the top of the canopy to the left again; it's all clear.

Watch the attitude through the windscreen as I roll into the turn. This is a medium turn to the left. See where the horizon cuts, from the top left corner to just above the compass; also note that the spinner appears just on the horizon because of the offset seating. Remember this attitude. We do not trim in the

turn, but to stay level you need to hold a slight back pressure on the stick. I will now hand over control to you so that you can feel the pull required. You have control."

STUDENT PRACTISES

"Good".

"I have control. You can also see that the speed has decreased by 5 Kts. We accept this loss as it is small. Finally fix the attitude in your mind. I will roll level. That was a turn to the left, so let's dissect it as in the briefing.

I will demonstrate an entry to the left, follow me through. Lookout as before, to the left, through the nose to the right and back over the top to the left; it's clear. Now look through the windscreen and immediately we enter the turn. Smoothly apply left aileron and co-ordinate this with a touch of left rudder as we roll. To stop descending, use enough back pressure to hold the nose position on the horizon. Approaching the turn attitude, check the roll with aileron and centralise the rudder. Here we are in a medium turn to the left.

Rolling level again, I want you to enter a turn to the left. I will then take control and demonstrate rolling out of the turn. Any questions?"

STUDENT ANSWERS.

"You have control."

STUDENT PRACTISES.

"I have control. Follow me through. To recover from the turn, roll the wings level with aileron, co-ordinate this with a touch of right rudder and, at the same time, relax the back pressure on the control column to keep the nose position relative to the horizon. Now check that we are straight and level again; so wing tip, nose, wing tip, it looks correct and this is confirmed on the instruments.

Just to clarify why we use rudder on entry and rollout, clamp your feet firmly on the rudder pedals and watch the nose. I will apply full left aileron and I want you to tell me which way the nose first moves."

STUDENT ANSWERS.

"Yes, it moved to the right. This is why we co-ordinate rudder with aileron when we roll the aircraft, on the entry and the recovery in turns. The term used to describe the movement is 'adverse yaw due to aileron'."

When I give you control practise an entry and recovery to the left and then put the aircraft into a further turn to the left. We can then have a look in detail at control in the turn. You have control."

STUDENT PRACTISES.

"I have control. Follow me through. In the turn, lookout is the first priority; never allow the mechanics of flying to take precedence over lookout. Secondly, we check our attitude is correct and confirm this with a glance at the instruments, bank 30°, altimeter level and slip-ball central. Then back to the lookout, attitude and confirmation on instruments, a continuous process.

Now let us change the visual attitude so we can have a look at making corrections. You can see the attitude is wrong and a check inside shows we have nearly 40° of bank. Visually adjust the bank to 30° with aileron, and a check on the artificial horizon confirms we're correct. Similarly, with height corrections, look — the nose is well below the horizon and the altimeter shows we're descending. Applying up elevator, raise the nose to its correct position; keep the bank angle constant. A check of the altimeter confirms we're level. Finally, we must ensure we are in balance and, as in straight and level flight, use the slip ball.

Rolling level, I want you to practise a few turns to the left. Remember in the briefing I stressed the importance of holding the bank steady and adjusting the height with elevator. There is only one back pressure for each angle of bank. You have control."

STUDENT PRACTISES.

"I have control. I will now demonstrate a turn to the right. Follow me through. Lookout is just the same but start by looking to the right first, round through the nose to the left and back over the top, to the right again. All is clear.

Entry is the same, using aileron and rudder to roll to this attitude, not forgetting the back pressure. This is the picture you want; the horizon runs across the windscreen from the top right corner to just below the compass. However, this time note that the spinner is lying just below the horizon, because your seat is offset slightly higher in the turn.

Now continue this turn and roll out when I ask you to. After that, practise a few more turns, alternating right and left, but don't forget to look out. You have control."

STUDENT PRACTISES.

"I have control. Good, you have mastered the basic technique and we can finish the exercise by rolling out on given headings. When I give you control, enter a turn to the left and bring the DI into your scan. As we pass 270° start a smooth roll out; we'll note the number of degrees required to regain straight and level. You can then use that knowledge to roll out on given headings. You have control."

STUDENT PRACTISES.

END OF EXERCISE.

EXERCISE 9 — MEDIUM TURNS — CLIMBING AND DESCENDING

Aircraft Position in Flight Profile

The aircraft is in a wing level straight climb at 80 Kts. The student has already been taught medium turns.

Air Exercise

"Here we are in a steady climb at 80 Kts. with a rate-of-climb of 700′ per minute. As I said on the ground, the difference from level turns is that in the climb we use 15° of bank and instead of holding our height, we keep the speed constant. I will demonstrate a climbing turn to the left, follow me through.

Look to the left, round the front to the right, and most important, up above and finally to the left again. To enter the turn, apply aileron plus a little rudder and check the angle of bank at 15°. I have also lowered the nose attitude slightly to hold 80 Kts.

This is the correct attitude for a climbing turn to the left, 15° of bank, 80 Kts. and in balance. You can see that we're

climbing at 500′ per minute, a decrease of 200″ per minute from the straight climb. Also, you may notice that we have to use a bit more opposite aileron to prevent the bank increasing.

In the turn, we use the same scan as for level turns, lookout, check the attitude and then confirm on the instruments that we have 15° of bank and 80 Kts., adjusting if necessary. I will roll out on 180°, using 10° anticipation. 190° coming up, so roll the wings level, a touch of right rudder and raise the nose a fraction to the straight climbing attitude.

Carry out a climbing turn to the left through 180°. Then using the same technique, try a turn to the right. You have control."

STUDENT PRACTISES.

"I have control. In the briefing I emphasised that we limit the bank used in climbing turns to preserve the rate of climb. Let's have a look at the effect of too much bank on our rate of climb. You can see that at this height we have a wings level climb of 650' per minute.

Follow me through. Looking out to the right, enter a climbing turn. Stabilising at 15° of bank, note the rate of climb is 500' per minute. Increasing the bank further to 45°, lower the nose to hold 80 Kts., and you can see the VSI only shows 300' per minute. Increase the bank even more to 65° and look — the nose is on the horizon and at this speed we are barely climbing.

Recovering to level flight, I think that is a fairly convincing demonstration that you must limit the bank used in climbing turns to maintain a reasonable rate of ascent.

I will now show you descending turns. Follow me through. Here we are in a glide at 80 Kts. with a rate of descent of 700′ per minute. Looking out to the left, round to the right and back to the left again, especially check that it is clear below. To enter the turn apply aileron with a touch of left rudder and lower the nose a fraction to maintain the speed. Check the bank attitude at 30°; we can afford a higher angle than in the climb. Use the

same priority of scan, lookout, attitude and then check inside to confirm 30° of bank, 80 Kts. and the ball central. Speed corrections are the same as in a straight descent; make positive pitch attitude changes.

You can see the rate of descent has increased to 900′ per minute, and you may also notice that we are hardly using any opposite aileron to maintain the bank.

I will roll out on West. 285° coming up, so rolling out smoothly with aileron and rudder together, raise the nose slightly to the straight gliding attitude. As we have not trimmed in the turn, the aircraft maintains the correct gliding attitude.

I would like you to try a turn to the left. Roll out on North, and then try a turn to the right on to South. First, however, what should we do periodically?"

STUDENT ANSWERS.

"Yes, warm the engine. You have control."

71

STUDENT PRACTISES.

"I have control. When I covered climbing turns, I showed you how the rate of climb decreased with increasing bank. Now, let us have a look at the effect of increasing bank in a descending turn. Look out to the right to check it's clear and roll into the turn. Stabilising at 30° of bank, check 80 Kts. and a rate of descent of 900' per minute.

Now, increasing the bank further to 45° and lowering the nose to hold 80 Kts., the rate of descent is nearly 1100' per minute. Going further to 60° of bank and, look, we're up to 1250' per minute. Increase the bank a little further and there's the stall warning horn. I will recover to the level cruise.

I hope that has convinced you of two things. You should restrict your bank if you are gliding for range and, more important perhaps, if you use an excessive amount, you will stall, even if your speed is correct; you will see the significance of this later on.

Now carry out some further turns, but this time lower half flap; use 80 Kts. and vary the power to control the rate of descent. You have control."

STUDENT PRACTISES

END OF EXERCISE.

EXERCISE 10 — STALLING — PART I

NOTES: (1) The sequence varies slightly from some conventional manuals, as the wing drop and the 'G' stall have been brought forward of the demonstration with flap. It is more logical, and most instructors seem to prefer this order.

(2) It is suggested that the carburettor heat is better left in cold during the final approach to the stall, in order to make recovery more realistic. It should, however, be regularly exercised before each stall. This is a suggestion rather than a dogmatic procedure.

(3) Some aircraft, e.g. the Cessna 150, cannot always be induced to drop a wing in the expected direction at the stall by the use of crossed controls.

(4) With a few aircraft, the control column may be fully back without the nose or the wing dropping. From a practical control point of view, the aircraft is stalled, although aerodynamically this may not be strictly true.

(5) This is the first exercise, as mentioned in the Preface, where the patter can be difficult to co-ordinate with the flying, e.g. the recovery action. It is, therefore, more of an abbreviated commentary than an explanation.

Aircraft Position in Flight Profile

Aircraft at 4000′ in straight and level flight at cruising speed. The student has revised medium turns satisfactorily.

Air Exercise

"I have control. The main exercise today is stalling, as we briefed on the ground. First we must complete the HASELL checks; I will carry them out this time. However, in future I'll expect you to know them perfectly: H stands for height. When solo you must have sufficient height to recover by 3000′ AGL. We allow 500′ to complete the manoeuvre and on top of this we must take into account the ground height over which we are flying. In this area 200' is the maximum. This gives us a minimum entry height of 3700', say 4000' on the QNH for this exercise. A is for airframe. Check that the flap is up, unless we deliberately intend to stall with flap down. Also, make sure that the brakes are off. Some aircraft have brake systems that restrict the rudder pedal movement if they are on. Finally cage the DI and artificial horizon if applicable. S stands for security. We check the cockpit to make sure that all loose articles, such as maps and pencils are stowed securely. Check your harness is tight and, finally, confirm that the canopy is locked. E is for engine. Check that oil temperatures and pressures are in the green. Select the fullest tank and switch on the fuel pump. Set mixture rich, and exercise the carburettor heat control, like this. Pull it out fully to the hot position for 10 secs. — now put it in fully to cold. L is for location. Make sure that you are not over either an active airfield or a built-up area. In addition, we must remain clear of controlled airspace. Pick an anchor feature so that you do not drift downwind in the exercise or become disorientated. We will use that square wood at 9 o'clock. L for lookout. We must carry out a lookout turn to clear the immediate area before each manoeuvre. Remember the briefing: we use either two 90° turns, say right and then left, or a single 180° turn. We can also use the turns to help us maintain our position near the 'anchor' feature.

We will start by having a look at the symptoms leading up to the stall. First the lookout. Follow me through. I will do two 90° turns. Look to the left first and pick a feature on the ground which is adjacent to the wing tip; we will use that wood to roll out on. Turning to the left, search above, level, and very important, below. There is the feature coming up, so rolling out now look to the right, pick another feature off the right wing tip, and turn towards it. Once again clear the area above, level and below.

Rolling out on our feature and, whilst the lookout is still valid, I will enter the stall, like this. First exercise the carb. heat — now throttle back to idle, check the yaw with rudder, and hold this height, 4000' by progressively raising the nose as the speed decreases. Keep the aircraft in balance with left rudder. The symptoms of the approaching stall are decreasing airspeed, sloppy, less responsive controls, and the higher nose attitude. Trim down to 70 Kts. There is the stall warning horn at 64 Kts. Continue to raise the nose, with the stick coming back as the speed decreases. I can now feel the buffet through the control column and finally, the airframe. At 56 Kts., the nose drops, even with the stick well back. We have stalled. I will let the aircraft descend and I want you to feel the buffet and remember it. Recovering now, I will climb back to 4000'.

You saw the symptoms leading up to a stall. Because I held the aircraft level the speed decreased and we had a high nose attitude.

Also the controls became sloppy and finally we had the warning horn followed by the airframe buffet, just before the nose dropped at 56 Kts., the actual point of stall.

We do not need to do the complete HASELL checks between each stall but instead, use the mnemonic HELL, an abbreviated form to jog our memory of important items such as height and fuel.

We check: H for height — confirm that our height will be valid — we are climbing again to 4000'. E for engine — fuel sufficient and balanced — T.'s and P.'s in the green. L for location — check our anchor feature — there it is at 11 o'clock. L for lookout — we must do this before each manoeuvre.

When I give you control. I want you to complete a thorough lookout and set the aircraft up for a further stall. I will take control at 70 Kts. and show you the stall itself. Remember to exercise the carb. heat before closing the throttle. From now on you will see me doing this automatically before each stall. Do you understand?"

STUDENT ANSWERS

"You have control."

STUDENT PRACTISES.

"I have control. Follow me through. There is the horn at 64 Kts. The stick is still coming back and the nose is rising to hold level flight. 60 Kts., feel the light 'burble'. 57 Kts., the buffet is heavier, and there goes the nose down at 56 Kts. We are stalled and sinking rapidly. Look at the rate of the descent, 1500' per minute. Recovering now. We have lost a lot of height, about 800'. Clearly we should recover earlier rather than sit in the stall.

I now want you to climb back to 4000' and then set the aircraft up for a further stall. I will take control at 70 kts. and show you a recovery without power. Do not forget a HELL check. Have you any questions?"

STUDENT ANSWERS

"You have control."

STUDENT PRACTISES.

"I have control. Follow me through. Look, we are at 4000', speed decreasing through 65 Kts. — 60 Kts., feel the light buffet — 56 Kts., heavy buffet and there goes the nose. Recovery — stick forward to lower the nose to this position —

buffet stops — speed increasing, so level the wings, and keep the ball in the middle — at 70 Kts. level out and increase the power. We are at 3600', so we lost 400' during the recovery.

Now, climb back to 4000', do not forget the checks and lookout. Then repeat a stall and recovery without power. You have control."

STUDENT PRACTISES.

"I have control. Well done. The next stall we will have a look at, is the recovery using power. Take the aircraft back to 4000' and, as before, set it up for another stall. Use a 180° lookout turn, so we can go back towards our anchor feature. You have control."

STUDENT PRACTISES.

"I have control. Exactly the same symptoms, decreasing airspeed and higher nose. The horn at 64 Kts., buffet starting at 60 Kts. and 56 Kts., pitching nose down. Recovery — stick forward, full power — check the yaw — see the nose position, it is not so low —

— buffet has stopped — speed increasing, so level the wings — 70 Kts., easing into a shallow climb, and look, we have lost only 200′. A better recovery with half the height loss; that is the standard stall recovery.

Notice that when I applied full power, I checked the yaw with right rudder. Also, just as important, I held the recovery attitude against the nose-up change of trim until the speed increased; try to anticipate this if you can. Remember you recover because you reduce the wing angle of attack by forward movement of the control column. Adding power decreases the time it takes to accelerate to a safe speed in a flatter descent. This results in a reduced height loss. You must recover as soon as you recognise any symptom of a fully developed stall; that is, when the buffet is heavy, when the nose drops or, when either a wing drops or the control column is fully back. I will cover the wing drop case later on.

I now want you to practise some fully developed stalls, using the standard stall recovery I have just shown you. Is that clear?"

STUDENT ANSWERS

"You have control."

STUDENT PRACTISES.

"I have control. I will now show you a wing drop at the stall. This does not happen often with modern aircraft in a clean configuration, so I will deliberately induce a wing drop to the left with rudder. Follow me through.

Turning through 180° to keep the wood in sight, it all seems clear. Now, rolling out, throttle back as before. Wait for the horn. There it is, 64 Kts., so feeding on some left rudder and keeping the wings level with aileron, watch the nose — down and rolling left.

Recovery — stick forward, full power, opposite rudder — speed increasing, level the wings with aileron — centralise the rudder — 70 Kts., ease out of the dive into a shallow climb.

Remember, do not use aileron to correct a wing drop at the stall. With some aircraft you could aggravate the situation. Instead, apply sufficient opposite rudder to the wing that has dropped to prevent yaw.

I now want you to practise a stall and recovery. I will override the rudder to induce a wing drop. Is that clear?"

STUDENT ANSWERS

"You have control."

STUDENT PRACTISES.

"I have control. In the briefing I also covered the accelerated, or 'G' stall, as it is sometimes called. I will set the aircraft up for a further stall. However, I will recover without using power so you can see clearly what happens. Follow me through.

Looking out again, 90° left, now 90° right; it is all clear. Throttling back, wait for the stall — there it is; recovering — watch the speed — 70 Kts., pulling out harshly — there is the buffet again — relax the back pressure to stop the buffet. Now full power to complete a normal recovery.

You could see that we stalled above the basic stalling speed because I pulled back too hard. If you encounter buffet during recovery, relax the back pressure until it stops. I would like you to repeat that yourself. You have control."

STUDENT PRACTISES.

"I have control. We will complete the exercise by looking at the recovery at the incipient stage. As I said in the briefing, 'incipio' means 'I begin', so an incipient recovery should be initiated at the first aerodynamic warning of the stall which, for the purpose of this exercise, we will consider to be the first sign of the buffet. However, in practise, it should be taken when the stall warner sounds a continuous note. The object of the exercise, then, is to recognise an approaching stall early on and then immediately recover, with the minimum loss of height. Follow me through.

Updating the HELL check, we are still at 4000′, the engine T.'s and P.'s are in the green, fuel sufficient, and I can see our anchor feature at 10 o'clock. Finally the lookout; I will carry out a 180° turn this time. It all seems clear, so rolling out and throttling back, we will hold 4000′. The symptoms are the same. 64 Kts. the horn; we ignore it — 60 Kts., the light buffet, so recovering — stick slightly forward, full power — chcck the yaw — notice I have hardly lowered the nose, about 2″ — 70 Kts., so ease into a climb. We have only lost 50′, a better recovery.

80

As I mentioned before, in reality do not ignore the warning horn; recover when you hear a steady note. In turbulent conditions it will sound intermittently. However, initially we will train to recover as soon as you feel the light buffet.

I would like you to finish the exercise practising incipient recoveries. Have you any questions?"

STUDENT ANSWERS

"You have control."

STUDENT PRACTISES.

END OF EXERCISE.

EXERCISE 10 - STALLING — PART II

NOTES: (1) In order to validate comparison, the initial power-on stall should be in level flight.

(2) To accommodate the patter, it is better if flap is lowered before closing the throttle.

(3) The final demonstration, the departure stall, should highlight the wisdom of recovering to an attitude.

Aircraft Position in Flight Profile

The student has completed satisfactory recoveries from fully developed and incipient clean stalls. He has completed the HASELL checks and the instructor has control.

Air Exercise

"We will now have a look at the effect of power on the stall. Instead of closing the throttle completely I will set 1500 RPM. Follow me through.

First I will carry out a 180° clearing turn — it all seems clear. Rolling out and throttling back to 1500 RPM, you can see that the speed decreases more slowly, but I still have to raise the nose to maintain height. Trim down to 70 Kts. Moving the controls, feel the ailerons — they are quite sloppy, but the rudder and elevator are firmer because of the extra slipstream. 62 Kts., the horn; the nose is just a fraction higher. The speed is trickling back. 56 Kts., feel a faint tremor — 53-52 Kts., there goes the right wing — recovering — full power, stick forward to lower the nose — opposite rudder — level the wings — centralise the rudder and easing into a shallow climb.

The main differences with power on compared to idle, is a slightly higher nose position, a 2 Kt. reduction in stall speed and, with this aircraft, the right wing tends to drop. Notice I did not hesitate to use full power during the recovery.

I would like you to do a similar stall and recovery. Do not forget to update the HELL check. You have control."

STUDENT PRACTISES.

"I have control. We will now look at the effect of flap, in two stages, half and fully down. Follow me through.

Turning through 180° to hold our position, it all seems clear. Checking that we are below 100 Kts., the flap limiting speed, lower half flap. Now throttle back to idle, raise the nose to hold level flight and retrim down to 65 Kts. 70 Kts., you can see that the nose is lower than with a 'clean' aircraft, and the speed is decreasing more quickly. 65 Kts. still no horn — 57 Kts., there is the horn — 52 Kts., feel the light buffet — 49 Kts. — the nose drops — recovering — stick forward, full power, check the yaw — nose in this position — speed increasing — 60 Kts., so level the wings and raise the nose into a gentle climb, like this. Hold this attitude to allow the speed to build up, and, now, at 80 Kts., raise the flap.

Notice that we stalled at 49 Kts., a lower speed than when the aircraft is clean. Also the nose was slightly lower on the horizon.

I would now like you to repeat the stall with half flap. Then set the aircraft up for a further stall and I will show you one with full flap. You have control."

STUDENT PRACTISES.

"I have control, follow me through. It is all clear, so checking we are below 100 Kts., lower full flap. Now throttle to idle, check the yaw, and, holding the height, look how quickly the speed is decreasing. Stop trimming at 65 Kts. — 54 Kts., there is the horn and the stick is still coming back — 49 Kts., feel the start of the buffet — 46 Kts., the stall — recovering — full power, stick forward — rudder to balance — level the wings with aileron — 60 Kts., ease the aircraft into level flight. We are hardly accelerating, so immediately raise the drag flap to half. Now increase the speed to 80 Kts. before raising the flap fully up. 80 Kts., so flap up and we can climb back to 4000'.

In reality there is little difference between the actual stalls with flap down, but it is important to note the slow rate of acceleration on recovery. Clearly, full flap has little effect on the stall speed, but keeping it fully down longer than necessary, could in some circumstances prejudice the recovery.

I want you to practise a full stall and recovery and then try some at the incipient stage, both with half and full flap selected. You have control."

STUDENT PRACTISES.

"I have control. Let us now apply our knowledge of the effect of power and flap on the stall, to the practical case. We will simulate a badly executed approach to land. Updating the HELL checks; our height is still good at 4000', fuel is sufficient and the engine T.'s and P.'s are in the green. Location, I am almost over the old airfield, and lookout, so turning through 180° to clear the area — I cannot see any other aircraft. Follow me through.

First set the aircraft up in a typical approach configuration, with full flap — 1400 RPM and 75 Kts. Imagine the visibility is bad; there is no horizon. We are searching for the runway and, inadvertently raising the nose, fail to notice the decaying airspeed. We ignore the stall warner, we have heard it all before, but our basic training is good. Suddenly, we feel the buffet — recovery — stick forward, full power — check the yaw — wings level — speed 60 Kts., nose on horizon — drag flap up — retrim, and continue with the climb to raise half flap at a safe height.

Now you try a similar stall and recovery from the incipient stage. You have control."

STUDENT PRACTISES.

"I have control. In reality, we must not ignore the warning horn, and later on we will use it as the point at which to recover.

Let us look at stalling in a turn; it might occur when turning on to the final approach. Follow me through.

Checking the speed is below 100 Kts., set half flap. Now commencing a turn through 180°, reduce the power to 1500

84

RPM and, raising the nose, allow the speed to decay. There is the horn at 60 Kts., higher than normal. Raising the nose even more, there is the buffet at 52 Kts. — recovery — stick forward, full power — rudder to balance — roll the wings level and smoothly ease into a shallow climb. Wait for 80 Kts. and, above 200', raise the flap as before.

Stalling in the turn is obviously dangerous, especially in the circuit. It is essential to roll the wings level as soon as the buffet stops; you must direct the lift upwards as quickly as possible.

I now want you to try a few similar stalls during a turn. First recover at the buffet, and then at the steady note of the horn, as you would if it occurred in the circuit. Is that clear?"

STUDENT ANSWERS

"You have control."

STUDENT PRACTISES.

"I have control. Finally, I will demonstrate the recovery from the climbing turn. It is sometimes called 'the departure stall', as it could happen when climbing out after take-off. Follow me through.

First the lookout, 90° right — now 90° left — it is all clear. Selecting half flap and 75% power, commence a climbing turn to the left like this. The horizon is obscured and ignoring the stall warner, we inadvertently allow the speed to fall. There is the buffet, recovery — stick forward, full power — notice the nose position — check the yaw — speed increasing, wings level — ease to the climbing attitude — speed 80 Kts., raise the flap. Did you take note of the nose position?"

STUDENT ANSWERS

"Yes, I lowered it to the position for the incipient stall recovery for level flight. If I had checked the nose when the buffet stopped, the aircraft would almost certainly have stalled again. Most light aircraft do not possess the power to accelerate with the nose high. You might be able to do it with fine flying at height, but at low level it is better to be safe than sorry. Notice, also, that despite the high power setting, I still did not hesitate to use full power.

Now try a similar stall and recovery from a climbing turn to the right. You have control."

STUDENT PRACTISES.

"I have control. You can see it is not quite so easy as a normal stall recovery; a salutary lesson perhaps, of reality.

That is the end of the stalling exercise, but it is so important that I will be asking you to practise incipient recoveries any time from now on."

END OF EXERCISE.

EXERCISE 10 — SLOW FLIGHT

NOTE: This exercise is given using a speed 10 knots above the stall, clean and with full flap set. The exercise may be repeated at the stall speed plus 5 knots. However, from a practical point of view most stall warning horns preclude "pattering" once they have been activated.

Aircraft Position in Flight Profile

The student has completed the HASELL checks and carried out a clean stall and recovery, the aircraft is back at 100 knots and the instructor has taken control.

Air Exercise

"You saw that the aircraft stalled at 55 knots at this weight. Now, follow through on the controls.

Here we are at the normal cruise speed with the nose about 6″ below the horizon. First the ailerons, rolling left, note the roll rate and response and now to the right. Similarly a small rudder input left and right, again see the response. Finally easing the stick forward and backwards. I want you to make the same control inputs when I give you control and to remember both the rate and the force as a reference. You have control."

STUDENT PRACTISES.

"I have control, completing a HELL check, height still good, E for engine — oil Ts and Ps good and check the carburettor heat — 2300 RPM, and 2100 RPM and back in, 2300 RPM, L for location, still near our wood and we'll lookout by turning through 180°.

All clear and rolling out. I will now reduce the speed to 65 knots. So setting 1650 RPM, keeping the aircraft in balance with rudder and raising the nose to hold the height. Here we are coming up to 65 knots, a touch more right rudder to keep us in balance. We're still level, retrimming, the nose is higher than at 100 knots.

So here we are 10 knots above the stall. Follow through on the controls. Moving the rudder — left and right — see the sluggish rate of yaw. Now the elevator — stick back and forward, again a slow response. Finally aileron to the right, see the slow roll rate and now to the left, there's the horn.

At this speed we are close to the stall and when we rolled, the horn was triggered. So at low speed in level flight the nose is higher, the controls are less responsive and the force required to move the controls lower.

I want you to try gentle control movements and compare them with those at cruising speed. You have control."

STUDENT PRACTISES.

"I have control. So what did you think of the control response."

STUDENT ANSWERS.

"Yes, the response was poor, but still normal and the control forces are lower. Let us now look at turning. Follow through on the controls.

Lookout and rolling to the right and stop there at 20°. Holding the height, see the speed has reduced slightly. Increasing the bank further, there goes the stall warning again. So easing forward to regain the speed and rolling out. I want you to try a turn to the left; roll to a low angle of bank and hold it for a few seconds, then increase the bank slowly until you trigger the stall horn. As soon as you hear the horn ease forward on the stick to recover as I did. Have you any questions?"

STUDENT ANSWERS.

"Good, well you have control."

STUDENT PRACTISES.

"I have control. So you can see that although you can turn at low speed, you are very close to the stall and must avoid turning at such low speeds.

Follow through on the controls. Let's lookout around and particularly up above. Now setting full power and raising the nose to maintain the speed; to keep the aircraft in balance we need quite a lot of right rudder and, of course, retrimming.

Here we are in a climb at a slightly lower rate than normal. Again checking the control response; rolling left and right — it is the same as in level flight. Onto the elevator, stick forward and back — a crisper response and firmer control. Similarly with the rudder — left and right. Clearly the extra slipstream over the tail feathers increases their response at low speed.

I will give you control so you can try the same control inputs. What will you do if the stall warning horn is triggered?"

STUDENT ANSWERS.

"Yes, lower the nose, you already have full power set. So you have control."

STUDENT PRACTISES.

"I have control. Throttling back to 1650 RPM and lowering the nose back to level flight. I'll check the carburettor heat again, hot air out — 1500 RPM — back in and restored to 1650 RPM.

We'll now check the handling in a descent with the power at idle. Looking out, it is still clear. Hot air out, power to idle, lowering the nose to hold 65 knots and retrimming.

Here we are descending, the nose is higher than in a normal glide at 80 knots. You can see the rate of descent is just over

700 ft/min, a fraction higher than normal. Follow through on the controls.

Again a gentle roll left and right, we still have the slow response in roll. Onto the elevator — stick back and forward, it is quite sluggish. Finally the rudder — left and right, again it is sloppy; clearly the lower slipstream accounts for this.

We can fly at low speed at all power settings, but anytime you trigger the stall warning you must take standard stall recovery action. You are at the incipient stage of a stall and should recover to a safer, higher speed. So easing back on the stick slightly and there's the horn.

Full power and relaxing the back pressure and here we are at 70 knots, we have recovered.

Throttling back and settling down again in a glide at 65 knots. When I give you control, I want you to check the control response. Have you any questions?"

STUDENT ANSWERS.

"Fine, well you have control."

STUDENT PRACTISES.

"Good I have control. Well we can now have a look at slow flight with full flap set. Here we are at 65 knots, lowering full flap and increasing power to 2000 RPM. The stall speed with full flap is 10 knots lower than with flap up, so reducing the speed to 55 knots and retrimming.

Follow through on the controls. Watch the attitude and now rolling left and right, the response is similar to that with the flap up. Next the elevator, stick forward and back — a fraction firmer. Finally the rudder, left and right. The extra slipstream firms up the tail end controls. I want you to feel the control response in this configuration. You have control."

STUDENT PRACTISES.

"Good, I have control. Adding a little power and making a gentle turn to the left to lookout, especially below. It looks clear, so carburettor heat out and throttling back to idle. Now lowering the nose to hold 55 knots and here we are in a descent, retrimming.

Follow through on the controls. Again trying each control to check the response. Ailerons, left — and — right, the response is the same as in level flight. Now the elevator, stick forward and back — it is sluggish; and finally the rudder left and right, again the response is slow. I want you to check the response in the descent. You have control."

STUDENT PRACTISES.

"I have control. Good, well I want you to now set full power and put the aircraft into a climb holding 55 knots. Note the low rate of climb with the flap down then check the control response. Have you any questions?"

STUDENT ANSWERS

"I will take over when you have tried the controls. You have control."

STUDENT PRACTISES.

END OF EXERCISE.

EXERCISE 11 — SPINNING — PART I

NOTE: (1) Note that centralising the controls also includes the control column.

          (2) The recovery action patter in the main text is abbreviated to harmonise with the characteristics of average light aircraft. A more comprehensive one is added at the end of the exercise for suitable aircraft.

Aircraft Position in Flight Profile

The student has successfully completed a revision of stalling which included a recovery with a deliberately induced wing drop.

Air Exercise

"During the climb, we can carry out the HASELL checks. Some aircraft are limited by their weight and C of G; one should have checked this before take-off. Also remember the additional height requirement. For a 4-turn spin for this aircraft, allow 250' per turn, or 1000' total plus 1000' for the recovery. As we must have recovered by 3000' AGL, it is advisable to climb to 6000' to be on the safe side. With some aircraft, brakes can restrict rudder movement, so check they are off, and of course, the flaps should be up.

Continue the climb and at the same time carry out your checks. You have control."

STUDENT PRACTISES.

"I have control. The large wood at 10 o'clock will make a good anchor feature and I will now show you how to enter a spin to the left. Follow me through. To lookout, we turn to the right, searching above, level and in particular below. Now reverse the turn back towards the wood, still looking above, level, and below. There is the wood coming up again on the nose, so without wasting time, level the wings and enter for the spin. Closing the throttle, check the yaw with rudder and maintain height as we do for a stall. Trim down to 70 Kts. At 61

92

Kts., 5 Kts. above the stall, we will apply full left rudder and bring the control column fully back, holding it central, — entering now — nose high, the incipient stage — nose dropped — rotation stabilised, the spin has developed — speed steady

at 55 Kts. — losing height rapidly — recovering now — it has taken ¾ of a turn to stop.

Let us now climb up again to 6000'. How do you feel? It was not too bad, was it?"

STUDENT ANSWERS

"Don't hesitate to tell me if you feel unwell; it does take some getting used to, but spinning is a very necessary part of your training. Did you notice that during the spin, I held the controls firmly pro-spin, that is full rudder in the direction of the spin, control column hard back with the ailerons central?"

STUDENT ANSWERS

"Now continue the climb to 6000', complete your HELL checks and then carry out a spin to the left. After it has stabilised, I will take over again, but you continue to follow me through and I will demonstrate the recovery, after pointing out one or two further characteristics. Any questions?"

STUDENT ANSWERS

"Remember it is important to apply full pro-spin control and this requires a certain amount of determination. You have control."

STUDENT PRACTISES UNTIL SPIN STABILISES.

"I have control — look at the turn indicator, it is hard over to the left, showing the yaw — the airspeed is low — now the recovery — check throttle closed, turn indicator and speed — full opposite rudder — stick forward until spin stops — centralise controls — roll level — ease out of dive to level flight or climb — make it fairly positive to avoid exceeding the Vne and 'G' limitations.

Did you notice that the rate of rotation increased as I pushed the stick forward?"

STUDENT ANSWERS

"This is normal and indicates that the aircraft is in the process of recovering. Also, note that when the spin stopped, I immediately centralised the controls, in particular the rudder. If the spin has developed, try and check the turn indicator as it

94

will give you a positive indication of the direction of yaw. The speed is also important because if it is increasing, you are no longer in a spin but probably a tight spiral dive, which requires a different recovery action.

Now climb up again to 6000', and then enter a spin to the left. I will count the turns for you and tell you when to recover. We can then check the height loss. You have control."

STUDENT PRACTISES.

"I have control. Good, that was a 4 turn spin, plus $\frac{3}{4}$ of a turn for the recovery. We lost 1800', so our estimation for recovery height was safe. If you are feeling alright, climb up again and try a spin to the right. The only difference will be the indicated airspeed which will be higher because the pitot head is out on the left wing. You have control."

STUDENT PRACTISES.

"Well done, that is as far as we go today. In the next exercise we will look at the recovery at the incipient stage."

END OF EXERCISE.

SPIN RECOVERY ACTION (MORE COMPREHENSIVE — FOR SUITABLE AIRCRAFT).

"Close the throttle — check turn indicator and speed — full opposite rudder — ailerons neutral — stick forward progressively until spin stops — centralise controls — look to nearer horizon — speed increasing — roll level — ease out of dive to level flight — make it fairly positive to avoid exceeding the Vne or the 'G' limitations."

END OF EXERCISE.

EXERCISE 11 — SPINNING — PART II

NOTES: (1) Many Schools teach that the most practical incipient spin recovery is to centralise the controls, especially if the entry is dynamic, or above the normal stall speed. The exception is the wingdrop at the stall, when sufficient opposite rudder is applied to prevent further yaw. However it must be said that in practise, both authors instinctively use some opposite rudder, and that with some aircraft this can save half a turn on recovery.

Aircraft Position in Flight Profile

The student has completed a 4-turn spin and recovery. He is climbing the aircraft to 5000' and has just completed the HELL checks.

Air Exercise

"I have control. Fairly obviously if we do inadvertently spin, especially near the ground, we would not wish it to develop fully, so now let us look at the recovery at the incipient stage.

Follow me through on the controls. First, let us carry out the incipient recovery at the earliest stage of the spin, when the wing drops in level flight. Inevitably, autorotation will be relatively slow and the nose not too low. A final lookout and enter in the normal manner but I will apply pro-spin control 5 Kts. lower at 56 Kts., the point of stall. Here is the stall warner and at 56 Kts., stick back and right rudder now — wing drops — recovery — stick forward and opposite rudder — full power — speed increasing, level wings with the horizon — rudder central and enter the climb.

Notice I only applied a small amount of opposite rudder to the wing drop, sufficient to prevent any further yaw. Does this remind you of any other exercise?"

STUDENT ANSWERS

"Yes, it is the same as the wingdrop at the stall. Now practise this early incipient spin recovery. You have control."

STUDENT PRACTISES.

"I have control. Now let us go a little further. I will complete the first turn; this is still the incipient stage as the spin will not yet have stabilised.

Follow me through on the controls. HELL checks — Height sufficient — T.'s and P.'s in the green, fuel sufficient — location, there is our anchor point — and finally, a thorough lookout through 180° — it seems all clear. Now, level the wings, close the throttle, and hold 5000' as the speed decreases. At 61 Kts. apply full pro-spin controls — round we go — recovery — centralise controls, throttle closed — speed increasing, level the wings and regain level flight.

If the aircraft rotates beyond the initial wing drop but still in the incipient stage, it is better to centralise the controls. Also, note that we stopped spinning with the nose low, and therefore closed the throttle; this is important. The criterion of nose low and high is approximately 30° below the horizon, or about 2½ feet as seen from the cockpit of this aircraft. I will show you — just about like this.

I now want you to repeat what I have just done, but don't forget your HELL checks. Have you any questions?"

STUDENT ANSWERS

"You have control."

STUDENT PRACTISES.

"I have control. Now let us try some practical applications of this. Follow me through. Don't let us forget the lookout above and below — it's clear. Imagine that we are in a climbing turn to the left, like this, with 2300 RPM set. Maybe the vis. is bad and we inadvertently apply top or right rudder and continue to pull back on the control column — we 'flick' outwards — recovery — centralise controls — full power — speed increasing, so level wings and regain level flight. That was quite a quick recovery, wasn't it?"

STUDENT ANSWERS

"Note that I still used power because the nose was relatively high and that the best recovery action at the incipient stage is to centralise the controls. Now try a climbing turn to the right. It may be necessary to make a last-minute application of pro-spin controls to achieve autorotation. You have control."

STUDENT PRACTISES.

"I have control. You seem to have got the idea of that. Follow me through. Updating our HELL checks, we have height in hand — T.'s and P.'s and fuel satisfactory — our anchor point is straight ahead, so let us turn 90° to the left to clear the area and then back to the anchor point — all is clear.

Our final practical application is a descending turn, in this case to the left with some power applied, say 1500 RPM. For some reason we apply bottom or left rudder like this, and to prevent over-banking, we are forced to apply opposite aileron; the controls are crossed and we are well set up for a spin. We also try to pull the turn tighter. We 'flick' inwards — recovery — throttle closed — centralise controls — speed increasing, roll first to the nearer horizon — now pull to level flight. Once the speed is reduced, apply power.

Notice I took the power off during the recovery, as the nose was well below the horizon. Are you feeling alright?"

STUDENT ANSWERS

"Now try a descending turn to the right and an incipient spin and recovery. You have control."

STUDENT PRACTISES.

Well, that's the end of the spinning exercise. You are not allowed to spin solo during your P.P.L. course, but from time-to-time I will ask you to carry one out when dual. Have you any questions?"

STUDENT ANSWERS

END OF EXERCISE.

EXERCISE 12 — NORMAL TAKE-OFF

NOTE: (1) It is appreciated that it may be better to raise the nosewheel before positive rotation on rough surfaces and in the military environment.

Aircraft Position in Flight Profile

Aircraft at the holding point with the power and pre-take-off checks complete. The instructor has control.

Air Exercise

"Now that we have completed all the checks, we should do three things before requesting take-off. First check the wind direction; you can see from the windsock that it is blowing slightly across from left to right, but almost down the runway. Secondly make sure there are no aircraft on finals; do not just rely on the Air Traffic controller; there may easily be a non-radio aircraft coming into land which he has not spotted. Finally, check there are no aircraft on the runway. We can now ask for take-off:

      Springfield, Alpha Zulu ready for departure."

      "Alpha Zulu, clear to take-off. Wind 250°/12 Kts."

      "Alpha Zulu.

Follow me through. A final check of the approach, now throttle back, brakes off and taxy on to the runway without delay; as a matter of principle, always use the full length. Roll forward on the centreline for two or three yards to straighten the nosewheel, apply the brakes, and pick a feature at the end of the runway on which to keep straight during the take-off run. I will use the left side of that small copse. Do you see it?"

STUDENT ANSWERS

"Good, now holding the control column in the centre with the ailerons and elevator neutral, release the brakes, heels on the floor, and smoothly open the throttle fully — keep straight on the copse with rudder — now stick slightly back to relieve the nosewheel — check speed increasing, T.'s and P.'s and full power, 2300 RPM — I will rotate at 60 Kts. — rotating now — stick slightly back to raise the nose here, just above the horizon

— wings level with aileron — hold this attitude, remember it and allow the speed to increase to 80 Kts. Now raise the nose a bit more to hold the speed and trim the attitude. Check the ball is central and choose a point on the horizon to the left of the nose on which to maintain your heading. Now at 200′ raise the flap and retrim for 80 Kts. Check the engine T.'s and P.'s, the ball is central and that we are climbing on the runway centreline. Finally, and most important, keep a very good look out, especially above."

END OF EXERCISE.

EXERCISE 12 — TAILWHEEL TAKE-OFF

Aircraft Position in Flight Profile

Aircraft at the take-off point, checks complete and cleared for take-off.

Air Exercise

"Follow me through. The approach is clear, so holding the stick back, move on to the runway and roll forward to straighten the tailwheel. Notice the nose obscures the view, so look out of the left side and pick a reference point well down the runway. We can expect a swing to the left, especially when the tail comes up. Initially, keep the control column back and the ailerons central. Releasing the brakes, smoothly open to full throttle — anticipate the swing with right rudder — now, ease the stick forward to raise the tail and apply more right rudder — hold this attitude with the elevators. Check full

power and speed increasing — 60 Kts., a slight back pressure and we're airborne. Keep the wings level and hold this attitude. Check the ball is central and climb away at 75 Kts. Retrim, if necessary.

END OF EXERCISE.

EXERCISE 12 — CROSSWIND TAKE-OFF

Aircraft Position in Flight Profile

The aircraft is at the take-off point with checks complete. The circuit is right hand. The instructor has control.

Air Exercise

"Before asking for take-off clearance note the wind direction; you can see from the windsock, that it is coming from the left at about 40° and 20 Kts. It is quite strong, but I have already calculated that it is within the limits of the aircraft.

"Springfield, Alpha Zulu ready for departure."

"Alpha Zulu, you are cleared to take-off. Wind 230°/20 Kts."

"Alpha Zulu.

The approach is clear, so line up on the runway in the normal manner. During the take-off run, we can expect the aircraft to weathercock into wind and the left wing may rise, so I will use coarse left aileron to begin with, and gradually reduce to half aileron at rotation.

Follow me through. With full left aileron and stick neutral, release the brakes, heels on floor and open smoothly to full throttle — anticipate right rudder, don't use brake — check speed increasing and full power — now reduce to half aileron and stick slightly aft of neutral — for a clean lift-off, rotate firmly 5 Kts. higher at 65 Kts. — rotating now — airborne, the aircraft weathercocks into wind — balance with rudder and correct for drift by turning slightly further into wind with aileron, to track down the centreline of the runway. At 200' and 80 Kts. retract the flaps as usual, and continue the climb."

END OF EXERCISE.

EXERCISE 12 — FLAPLESS TAKE-OFF

Aircraft Position in Flight Profile

Aircraft at take-off point, checks complete.

Air Exercise

"I have control. I will now show you a flapless take-off, the significance of which only really applies to an aircraft normally scheduled to take off with flap down. Follow me through.

First, we should have checked that the runway is long enough, as the take-off roll will be longer:

> "Springfield, Alpha Zulu ready for departure."
> "Alpha Zulu, you are clear to take-off. Wind 260°/10 Kts."
> "Alpha Zulu.

The approach is clear, so we line up in the normal manner, using the full length of the runway. Apply full power on the brakes, check the temperatures and pressures, heels on the floor and we are away. Keep straight with rudder, stick slightly more aft than normal, we will rotate 5 Kts. higher at 65 Kts. and can expect a slightly higher nose attitude. Smoothly rotating now, nose on horizon, ball in the centre, wings level and we climb out as usual at 80 Kts.

Notice that my rotation was smooth to avoid a possible 'G' stall, and hitting my tail on the ground; however the main thing to remember is that the take-off run is longer."

END OF EXERCISE.

EXERCISE 12 — SHORT FIELD TAKE-OFF

NOTE:　(1) Maximum lift flap will not necessarily produce the shortest take-off distance to 50′, so the Flight Manual should always be consulted.

Aircraft Position in Flight Profile

Checks are complete at the take-off point. Maximum lift or half flap has been selected, which on this aircraft is recommended for a short field take-off.

Air Exercise

"I will now show you a short field take-off. I want you to imagine that the runway is a short farm strip with average length grass, which I have already checked in the Flight Manual is adequate. However, remember that the slope and the condition of the ground can dramatically affect the take-off run, especially with nosewheel aircraft:

"Springfield, Alpha Zulu ready for departure."

"Alpha Zulu, you are cleared to take-off. Wind 260°/10 Kts."

"Alpha Zulu.

The approach is clear so we taxy to the farthest downwind boundary of the airfield and turn into wind as close to the fence as reasonably possible. Initially we will hold the stick well aft of neutral to relieve the weight on the nosewheel, as the grass could provide quite a lot of drag, but as we gather speed we will relax it a little, otherwise the main wheels may sink into the ground and cancel out the advantage.

Follow me through on the controls. Now, holding the brakes on, open to full power, check temperatures and pressures and 2300 RPM. With the stick about here, release the brakes, heels on the floor and keep straight with rudder; as the elevator begins to 'bite' relax the back pressure slightly. If the acceleration is obviously poor abandon the take-off. At 55 Kts., make a fairly firm rotation like this, into a slightly higher than normal nose attitude — without overdoing it — so that the aircraft accelerates to the best angle of climb speed, of 71

106

Kts., which we maintain until we are clear of all obstacles —
now at 200′ AGL., increase the speed to 80 Kts., raise the flaps
and continue to climb."

END OF EXERCISE.

EXERCISE 12 — TAKE-OFF — ENGINE FAILURE AFTER TAKE-OFF

NOTE: (1) Some engine manufacturers do not recommend selecting carb. air hot, under these circumstances.

Aircraft Position in Flight Profile

The aircraft is climbing away on the extended centreline at 400' and 80 Kts. The instructor has control.

Air Exercise

"We always tell Air Traffic Control when we are going to practise an engine failure after take-off, otherwise they may initiate emergency action. Follow me through. I will simulate an engine failure by closing the throttle and as a safeguard, select carb. air to hot:

Springfield, Alpha Zulu fanstop."

"Alpha Zulu, Roger, call climbing away."

"Alpha Zulu.

Throttling back to idle, immediately lower the nose and trim for the glide at 80 Kts. Do not turn back at low level. Pick the best clear area ahead; I'll take the long field just to the left.

Crash checks; I will simulate them — Throttle closed, Mixture to idle cut-off, Fuel cock and pump off — Ignition off — Harness tight — Canopy unlocked — Warn the passengers.

Mayday, Mayday, Mayday, Alpha Zulu engine failure, force landing ahead.

We can make the field, so full flap and land as best you can. Overshooting now, call:

Alpha Zulu, climbing away."

"Alpha Zulu."

"You can see it all happens rather quickly and, in practice, we cannot cover every circumstance. Remember though, that the important point is to lower the nose promptly to hold the glide speed. Never turn back at low level, but choose the best area within a 30° arc either side of your flightpath. Carry out the crash checks as soon as possible. During practice, use touch drills, like this; just point out or touch the controls you are referring to. In reality you may find the fuel or ignition off, in which case it might be worth trying to get the engine re-started if you have height to spare. On the other hand, if you are too low, it might spoil your chances of making a forced landing. Also, if you have time, put out a Mayday call. Finally, remember you are not allowed to practise engine failure after take-off solo."

END OF EXERCISE.

EXERCISE 13 — NORMAL CIRCUIT

NOTES: (1) We have given 3 examples of patter for the final approach. The first is the general format, the second emphasises airspeed control and includes a roller landing, and the third is a more precise demonstration of glidepath control, which can only be accommodated on a longer than normal approach.

(2) It is recommended that a constant speed approach is taught in the early stage of training.

(3) During the landing phase, just before touchdown, the term 'keep straight with rudder' has been used. Strictly speaking, one should say 'keep the axis of the aircraft aligned with that of the runway.' Clearly, to patter this is impractical, nevertheless the connotation of the traditional phrase should be explained to the student during the briefing. Rudder, by itself, is never used to counteract drift.

(4) The use of carburettor heat may vary from the text, according to aircraft type.

Aircraft Position in Flight Profile

Aircraft is climbing after take-off, on the extended centreline of the runway. The instructor has control. The circuit is left hand.

Air Exercise

"We continue the climb at 80 Kts. on the centreline of the runway to 500', where we turn left on to the crosswind leg to track at 90° to the runway heading. 500' shortly coming up, so choose a turning point just forward of the left wing tip, to allow for the drift. Do you see that barn?"

STUDENT ANSWERS

"Looking for other aircraft joining the circuit, to the right, over the nose and to the left, we can turn left now, using 15° of bank; maintain 80 Kts. by slightly lowering the nose. There is the barn ahead, so rolling out, continue up to 1000′ at 80 Kts. During the climb, check behind to confirm that we are tracking at 90° to the runway. It is better to make too much allowance for drift than too little. We turn downwind when the tailplane lies over the runway, probably shortly after levelling at 1000′. 950′ coming up, so anticipate by lowering the nose smoothly into the level attitude, and allow the speed to increase. At 90 Kts., power back to 2200 RPM and trim precisely for level flight. Glancing back to the tail, it is over the runway, so first

look right for aircraft joining downwind, then back over the nose and to the left; it is all clear. Now, choosing a point just behind the left wing tip, make a level turn towards it, using 30° of bank.

We aim to roll out downwind, parallel to the runway, with the wing tip tracking down it. Try to do this visually, but the DI can help us; it should read 090°, the runway reciprocal, if there is no drift.

There is our reference point, so rolling out, check we are tracking correctly. You can see the wing tip is just on the runway, and the DI reads 090°. Now, opposite the upwind end of the runway, call:

Alpha Zulu, downwind."
"Alpha Zulu, cleared to finals, number one."
"Alpha Zulu.

Still tracking downwind and monitoring the height, we carry out our checks. Brakes off — Undercarriage down — Mixture rich — Carb. air hot; we have to raise the nose slightly to counteract the speed loss — Pitch fine — Fuel sufficient for overshoot, and pump on — Flaps up — Harness tight — Canopy secure — Carb. air cold.

Now, look at the runway to check our tracking. We appear to have drifted slightly, so we must turn 10° left, like this; sometimes you may have to 'dog-leg'. As we are going to practise a powered approach landing, wait until the runway threshold appears at 45° behind the left wing. This is about correct,

so looking to the right for aircraft joining crosswind, to the front and left, commence a level turn on to base leg, using 30° of bank. To allow for drift, we turn a bit more than 90°. Rolling out now, hold the attitude and immediately reduce power to 1500 RPM. Checking the speed is below 100 Kts., select half flap, lower the nose slightly and trim precisely for 80 Kts.

We aim to turn finals at about 600′ by adjusting the rate of descent on base leg, but 1500 RPM should suffice. You can use the altimeter to help your judgement, but it is better to learn the correct aspect of the runway, so look outside and try to remember it. Before turning finals, look right for other aircraft

on a longer approach; it is all clear. Now, anticipating with the nose on the extended centreline of the runway, start a turn on to the final approach. Adjust the angle of bank to suit but don't use more than 30°. Still maintain 80 Kts. by slightly lowering the nose. When we are almost in line with the runway, call:
        Alpha Zulu, finals."
        "Alpha Zulu, cleared to land. Wind 270°/10 Kts."
        "Alpha Zulu.
    Levelling the wings, lock the nose just short of the threshold, lower full flap and trim for 75 Kts. Note the aspect of the runway which we maintain by adjusting the rate of descent with power. The airspeed is controlled by making small, positive pitch changes with the elevators. The centreline is held with the use of aileron and the aircraft is kept balanced with rudder. All the way down monitor Runway — Airspeed — Runway and aim to cross the threshold at about 50′ at 75 Kts. I want you to note the flare which we initiate at about 20′ or the height of a double decker bus. Looking outside along the runway with the wings level, flare now.

    Throttle closed to hold off just above the ground, with the stick coming back and the nose rising — to touch down —

on the main wheels first — now gently lower the nosewheel —
keep straight with rudder and brake, if necessary with the stick
aft of neutral.

Now that the aircraft has almost stopped, first look left, and
then turn off the runway. When well clear, stop and carry out
the after-landing checks — Flaps up — Pitot heat off — Fuel
pump off — Slacken the throttle friction nut.

On the next circuit, I will show you how to recognise
deviations from the glidepath and how to regain it with power.
Speed control is basically done with the elevators, but if you
are certain that you are on the correct approach path, power
and elevator control cannot be separated. As a rough guide,
the nose should not vary very much from just short of the
threshold, until you are getting close to the boundary when it
moves forward to the touchdown point."

END OF EXERCISE.

Aircraft Position in Flight Profile

Aircraft is just about to complete the final turn on to the
approach. The instructor has control and will also
demonstrate a 'roller' landing and overshoot.

Air Exercise

"Levelling the wings, lock the nose just short of the runway
threshold. Now, without delay, lower full flap and trim for 75
Kts. This is the picture or aspect of the runway we want to see
all the way to the threshold. Also, note its position on the
windscreen; it should remain constant. Use aileron to maintain

the centreline of the runway, and hold 75 Kts. all the way in with the elevators. To increase speed, lower the nose slightly, hold the new attitude and trim. To decrease the speed, raise the nose a fraction, hold and trim. Only glance at the airspeed, the governing factor is attitude. We control the rate of descent with power, but more about that on the next circuit. Approaching the threshold, look how the nose has moved forward to the touchdown point, just beyond the numbers. Now, check heels on the floor, I want you to remember the flare. Look well down the runway and, with the wings level, flare now — throttle closed to hold off just above the ground, with the stick coming back and the nose rising, to touch down on the main wheels — now gently lower the nosewheel — keep straight with rudder with the stick slightly back.

To roll, check heels on the floor and open the throttle to full power, keeping straight with rudder. Check T.'s and P.'s, full power and speed increasing. We rotate slightly earlier at 55 Kts. — rotating now — nose slightly lower than normal to hold 70 Kts. Once we are trimmed and comfortably established in the climb like this, raise the drag flap to half, and continue the climb at 75 Kts. to 200'. You have control."

END OF EXERCISE.

Aircraft Position in Flight Profile

Aircraft on long finals, with full flap. The instructor has control, and has told the student that he will now demonstrate how to control the glidepath using a rather longer than normal approach.

Air Exercise

Deliberately reducing the power too much but holding 75 Kts., you can see the attitude is lower than before and the runway is moving up the windscreen; our rate of descent is too high. Now look at the runway — it is flatter; we are below the glidepath.

To regain it, increase the power and raise the nose to hold the speed. We are now back on the glidepath, but I will intentionally fly through it to put us high. The threshold has moved well down the windscreen and the runway appears steeper. Our rate of descent is too low and we are high on the glidepath.

To regain the correct approach path, reduce power slightly and lower the nose to hold 75 Kts. Here we are, back with the desired picture, and to hold it, I must add a little power like this, and simultaneously raise the nose a fraction to maintain 75 Kts. Don't forget to trim. Once you are steady on the glidepath, control the speed by making small pitch adjustments with the elevator. Approaching the flare, heels on the floor, look well down the runway — flaring now — close the throttle, keep straight with rudder, wings level with aileron — hold off — touchdown — gently lower the nosewheel — keep straight, and brake, if necessary, with the stick coming back.

We will turn off at the next intersection and after stopping I want you to carry out the after-landing checks."

STUDENT PRACTISES.

"I have control. Remember two things. First, when you correct the speed, don't follow the airspeed indicator, but instead concentrate on precise but small attitude adjustments by looking outside. Only glance at the airspeed indicator.

Secondly, don't allow pitch trim changes with power to override your attitude requirements. You should recall that when you apply power, the nose tends to rise and when you reduce power, the nose goes down."

END OF EXERCISE.

EXERCISE 13 — GLIDE APPROACH AND LANDING

NOTE: (1) In order to cover all the salient points, two demonstrations should be carried out.

Aircraft Position in Flight Profile

Aircraft at the beginning of the downwind leg. The circuit is right hand.

Air Exercise

"I have control. I will now show you a glide approach landing. The distance out on the downwind leg is standard, with the wing tip running down the runway. Call:
                Alpha Zulu downwind glide."
        "Alpha Zulu cleared to finals No. 1."
        "Alpha Zulu.
    It is important to know the wind, so ask A.T.C. if necessary. Checks are normal. Brakes off — undercarriage down — mixture rich — carb. air hot — pitch fine — fuel, sufficient for overshoot — pump on — flaps up — harness tight — canopy closed — carb. air cold. We don't go as far downwind as with a powered approach, but turn when the threshold is just behind the trailing edge to make a fairly tight base leg. Looking to the

left, around to the right, this is about correct, so using 30° of bank, make a level turn, a bit more than 90° to allow for the wind. Rolling out now, maintain the power until you are

certain of gliding a third of the way into the field. As a rough
guide, wait until the threshold appears at an angle of about 40°.
This will do, so closing the throttle, lower the nose and trim to

hold 80 Kts. all the way down to the flare. We aim to turn finals
at 600′ and this will help us judge our progress on base leg.
Now, as we are still certain of making the field, lower half flap
and trim for 80 Kts. In principle, don't use full flap until the
final approach; instead, vary the base leg by cutting the corner
towards the field if we are low, and turning away if we are high.
Before turning finals, look left and below for other aircraft.
Turning now, use about 30° of bank and maintain 80 Kts. by
lowering the nose. Rolling out on the centreline, call:

> Alpha Zulu finals."
> "Alpha Zulu you are cleared to land. Wind 260/10
> Kts."
> "Alpha Zulu.

Never try to stretch the glide; swallow your pride and add
power. Clearly we are comfortably going to make the field, so,
selecting full flap to bring the touchdown point closer to the
threshold, lower the nose even more and trim to hold 80 Kts.

Note the high rate of descent — we must flare early, so looking outside and with the wings level, flare now —

to hold off just above the ground — with the stick coming back and the nose rising — to touch down on the main wheels — now gently lower the nosewheel — keep straight with rudder and brake if necessary."

END OF EXERCISE.

EXERCISE 13 — GLIDE APPROACH LANDING (GLIDEPATH ASSESSMENT)

Aircraft Position in Flight Profile

Aircraft at the beginning of the downwind leg, after the intitial glide demonstration. The circuit is right hand.

Air Exercise

"I will now show you some 'tricks of the trade' to help you judge your glide approach. You fly the aircraft and I will talk you through it and tell you when to close the throttle and lower flap. I will also make the radio calls:

Alpha Zulu, downwind."

"Alpha Zulu, you are cleared to finals."

"Alpha Zulu.

Now you carry out the checks."

STUDENT PRACTISES.

"Have you noticed the drift?"

STUDENT ANSWERS.

"Yes, it is coming from the right which means we will have a headwind on base leg and must therefore delay closing the throttle.

Now turn onto base leg, where we will be able to get some idea of our drift and groundspeed. Incidentally, I hope you noticed that I was not deceived into delaying the turn, just because the wing was lying rather back.

Look outside and you can see we are making fairly slow progress, so we must not close the throttle too early. Also our drift is negligible and this tells us that we will have little or no wind on the final approach. We therefore must not turn finals too high or too close in.

We should be able to get in now, so close the throttle but do not lower flap until we have further assessed our progress.

We are still fairly high, so lower half flap and be prepared to fly through the centreline slightly, if necessary.

It is all clear to the left and 500' coming up so start the turn, but do not use too much bank as the wind will help us back. You can now see the aircraft beginning to accelerate over the ground, therefore lower full flap but remember to maintain your airspeed.

Alpha Zulu, finals."

"Alpha Zulu, you are cleared to land. Wind 210°/10 Kts."

"Alpha Zulu.

Now complete the approach and landing. You have control."

STUDENT PRACTISES.

END OF EXERCISE

EXERCISE 13 — CROSSWIND CIRCUIT AND LANDING (CRAB TECHNIQUE)

NOTE: (1) Except for aircraft that are clearly over-flapped for normal operations, there is no aerodynamic reason why flap selection should be restricted, except in severe wind shear conditions. On the contrary, with most modern aircraft, full flap enhances stability, can in some cases increase roll response for a given speed, and allows better glidepath control because of the extra power required, which is particularly applicable when the headwind component is small.

Aircraft Position in Flight Profile

The instructor has control shortly after take-off. The circuit is right hand and the crosswind is from the left.

Air Exercise

"As we will have a tailwind on the crosswind leg, we must delay turning until we are slightly higher than usual to ensure that we are not too far out on the downwind leg. 600' coming up, so, choosing a point abeam the right hand wing tip, commence a turn crosswind in the normal manner, although aim to roll out slightly later as the drift will be less.

Rolling out and almost immediately we have to level off at 1000', so reduce power to 2200 RPM, and trim. Look left and right, and without delay, turn downwind otherwise we will be blown too far out from the runway. To allow for the drift, continue the turn until the nose is angled towards the runway, like this;

now roll out. It is better to allow too much for drift than too little.

Alpha Zulu, downwind."

"Alpha Zulu, you are cleared to finals."

"Alpha Zulu.

Checks: brakes off — undercarriage down — mixture rich — carb. air hot — pitch fine — fuel on, sufficient for overshoot — pump on — flaps up — harness tight and canopy closed — carb. air cold.

The distance out from the runway should be the same as with the normal circuit, although the wing is pointing somewhat backwards. As the wind component down the runway is small, do not turn base leg too early. This will do with the threshold at about 45°, although be careful not to be deceived by the angle of the wing to the runway.

Checking left and right for other aircraft, commence a level turn aiming to roll out earlier than normal, as there will be little drift on base leg. Rolling out now, reduce power to a slightly higher setting than normal, because of the headwind; 1600 RPM should do. Lower half flap and trim for 80 Kts. We still aim for a straight-in approach from 4 to 500'. Do not anticipate the turn onto finals as much as usual, but wait until we are almost in line with the runway. Checking to the left for other aircraft —turn now aiming to roll out early with the nose pointing to the left of the runway to allow for the drift.

Alpha Zulu, finals."
"Alpha Zulu, you are cleared to land. Wind 230°/20 Kts."
"Alpha Zulu.

Rolling out now, lower full flap and trim for the normal approach speed of 75 Kts. Track down the centreline of the runway by off-setting the nose into wind with the use of aileron. Keep the aircraft balanced with rudder. Aim to cross the boundary at the usual height. The approach is normal except that we are crabbing down the centreline with the picture of the runway seen through the right-hand side of the windscreen. Keep it there with the use of aileron. It is better to

allow too much for drift than too little. With the threshold coming up, look outside to judge the flare and hold off. Just before touching down, I will ease the aircraft straight with rudder, and simultaneously apply opposite aileron to prevent roll. Flaring now — throttle closed to hold off —

stick coming back — now right rudder and left aileron to touch down straight on the main wheels — centralise the rudder and gently lower the nosewheel — still hold left aileron — anticipate right rudder to keep straight and if necessary, use brake.

Note that the moment of straightening the aircraft with rudder is critical for two reasons. If we do it late we will land sideways, and if we do it too early we will pick up drift and land across the runway. Don't try to force the aircraft on to the ground when it is still flying, as it will probably induce the worst type of 'wheelbarrowing'. Better to overshoot. Make up your mind early. Later I will show you an alternative method, the wing-down technique. With most aircraft it is easier, although some twin-engined aircraft have critical prop. clearances with the ground.

Now taxy back to the take-off point, make a further circuit and practise what I have just shown you. It is fundamental to crosswind landings. You have control."

STUDENT PRACTISES

END OF EXERCISE

EXERCISE 13 — CROSSWIND LANDING (WING-DOWN TECHNIQUE)

Aircraft Position in Flight Profile

The aircraft is on the final approach, with full flap selected, and the crosswind is from the left.

Air Exercise

"I have control. This time I will show you the wing-down technique. We aim to cross the hedge at the usual height but as we approach the threshold, apply right rudder to align the aircraft's axis with that of the runway and slight left bank with aileron to maintain the centreline, like this — continually

adjust the rudder to hold the aircraft axis with the runway, and use aileron to maintain the centreline with left bank. You can now see the runway is in the centre of the windscreen, but with slight left bank applied. Flaring now — hold off, still with right rudder and left bank to touch down on the left wheel first, then

the right, and finally lower the nosewheel. Keep straight with rudder, still holding left aileron.

The art is to gear your mind to use aileron to counteract drift. Now you show me a crosswind landing using the wing down technique. You have control."

STUDENT PRACTISES.

END OF EXERCISE

EXERCISE 13 — CROSSWIND CIRCUIT AND LANDING (COMBINATION WING-DOWN AND CRAB TECHNIQUE).

Aircraft Position in Flight Profile

Aircraft is turning downwind on a right hand circuit and the instructor has control. The runway direction is 270° but the wind is 320°/20 Kts. which will tend to drift the aircraft towards the airfield on the downwind leg.

Air Exercise

"The crosswind will be from the left on the downwind leg so we must stop the turn early to allow for the drift. Rolling out now.

It is better to allow too much than too little, especially as we have two further turns.

  Alpha Zulu downwind."

"Alpha Zulu, you are cleared to finals."

"Alpha Zulu.

Downwind checks: brakes off — undercarriage down — mixture rich — carb. air hot — pitch fine — fuel, sufficient for overshoot — pump on — harness tight and canopy closed — carb. air cold.

We aim to turn base leg when the threshold is at 45°, but note that our right wing is leading along the runway which could deceive us into turning too early. If anything, it is better to

delay the turn because the wind component down the runway will be small. This will do, so looking left and right, make a 30° bank level turn. As we will have a tailwind we will have to work fast on base leg. Rolling out now, immediately lower half flap and reduce power to 1200 RPM, a lower setting than normal; we must make certain that we are not too high on finals. Trim for 80 Kts. Looking to the left to check for other aircraft, anticipate the final turn much earlier — better to overdo it than underdo it. Starting the turn now, if it does get too tight better to overshoot rather than risk a stall on finals. Already you can see that the wind is carrying us towards the centreline of the runway — maintain 80 Kts. and roll out well after the nose has passed through the centreline to allow for drift from the right.

Alpha Zulu finals."

"Alpha Zulu, you are cleared to land. Wind 320°/20 Kts."

"Alpha Zulu.

Rolling out, immediately lower full flap and do not hesitate to take off power if we are too high on the glidepath. Imagine there is zero wind down the runway. Now, crab down the centreline, using aileron. We will do a combination crab and wing down technique, and roll the wings level just before touchdown. Aim for the normal threshold height and just before the flare, apply left rudder like this, to yaw the nose in line with the runway and right bank to maintain the centreline

— flaring now — throttle to idle — hold off — now wings level and centralise rudder — touch down on the main wheels — now gently lower the nosewheel — anticipate left rudder to keep straight and brake if necessary."

END OF EXERCISE

EXERCISE 13 — FLAPLESS CIRCUIT AND LANDING

Aircraft Position in Flight Profile

Aircraft at the start of the downwind leg. The circuit is right hand.

Air Exercise

"I will now show you a flapless approach and landing. We track downwind in the normal manner, with the wing tip on the runway. We call:

Alpha Zulu, downwind flapless."

"Alpha Zulu, cleared to finals number two."

"Alpha Zulu.

Now you carry out the pre-landing checks please."

STUDENT PRACTISES.

"Without the drag of the flap our final approach will be relatively flat, and we therefore fly farther downwind until the tailplane appears abeam the threshold. Also, we use 80 Kts. on the approach because our stall speed is higher. Now look well behind and you can see the tailplane is just coming abeam the threshold. Looking left and right, start a level turn on to base leg using 30° of bank. Rolling out to allow for drift, reduce the power, rather less than normal, to 1200 RPM and trim for 80 Kts. We aim to roll out on finals at the normal height of approximately 400', but, because we want to avoid tightening the final turn, anticipate a bit more than usual. Looking left, all seems clear, so rolling into the turn, maintain 80 Kts. by slightly lowering the nose.

As we roll out, call:

Alpha Zulu, finals flapless."

"Alpha Zulu, cleared to land. 260°/10 Kts."

"Alpha Zulu.

You can see that the runway appears much flatter; we look as if we are low. In fact this is the correct picture. You can also see that the nose is higher, and the runway more difficult to see. We peg the speed at 80 Kts., which is more sensitive to pitch changes. Also control of the rate of descent requires finer adjustment of the power.

As we are faster and clean, we will use more runway and therefore must try for a precise touchdown point. Approaching the boundary rather lower than normal, bring it into your approach path scan.

To avoid floating, we will reduce the power early and must be careful not to over-flare as we are almost in the landing attitude. Now throttle to idle, flare smoothly, with the stick coming back to touch down, nose high — now gently lower it, and brake, increasing as the speed decreases.

You can see the landing roll is longer than a normal landing with flap."

END OF EXERCISE

EXERCISE 13 — THE SHORT FIELD APPROACH AND LANDING

NOTE: (1) 1.3 the approach stall speed is the recommended threshold speed. It will vary with weight and, if correctly computed, will probably be less than most pilots use for a normal approach. However, it is doubtful whether most general aviation aircraft will be flying on the 'wrong side of the power curve'. Nevertheless, if the touchdown point is exact, the landing distance will be short.

Aircraft Position in Flight Profile

The instructor has taken over at the commencement of the downwind leg. It is a right hand circuit.

Air Exercise

"I have control. This time I will show you a short field landing. Follow me through.

Alpha Zulu downwind, short field landing."
"Alpha Zulu, you are cleared to finals, Number 1."
"Alpha Zulu.
Now complete the downwind checks whilst I fly."

STUDENT PRACTISES.

"Good. We turn on to base leg in the normal position with the threshold 45° behind. Looking left and right commence a level turn, using 30° of bank. Rolling out, as usual, to allow for the drift, lower half flap and reduce power to approximately 1300 RPM, slightly less than normal. This is to make certain that we are not too high on finals. Trim for 80 Kts. We should be lined up with the runway, no higher than 400', so adjust the base leg to turn finals at about 500'. Looking left — all is clear, so start the turn now. You can already see that the runway perspective is slightly flatter as we aim to cross the boundary at the minimum safe height, approximately 25' in this case. Rolling out, call:

135

Alpha Zulu finals."

"Alpha Zulu, you are cleared to land. Wind 270°/10 Kts."

"Alpha Zulu.

Now, lower full flap and initially trim for 75 Kts. Notice the slightly lower approach path, although the rate of descent is about normal. We aim to cross the boundary at our threshold speed of 60 Kts., to touch down as close to the boundary as reasonably safe. Now, about 250 yards short of the hedge, decrease the speed to 60 Kts. by reducing the power about 100 RPM and raising the nose slightly, about 2″ — 60 Kts., so add a bit of power to hold the rate of descent. Trim to lock the attitude. Hereafter, combine small pitch and power adjustments to hold the speed and flightpath. Now, at the threshold height, with the speed stabilised, look outside, to embrace the hedge and the touchdown point. Aim to flare with power on — flaring now — stick back — throttle closed — touchdown — lower the nose — firmly brake with the stick back — dab the brakes if you start to skid — check throttle closed — keep straight with rudder.

Now, taxy back to the take-off point and practise a short take-off, a circuit and short field landing. Remember two things. If you reduce power significantly during the approach, reapply it before the flare. Secondly, aim to stabilise the speed at 60 Kts. by the threshold height, then concentrate outside. If you have to make attitude changes at this stage, combine them with power and don't take too much off. You have control."

STUDENT PRACTICES

END OF EXERCISE

EXERCISE 13 — THREE-POINT LANDING (CONVERSION TO TAILWHEEL AIRCRAFT)

Aircraft Position in Flight Profile

The final turn has just been completed at 400'.

Air Exercise

"I have control. Follow me through. I will now show you a three-point landing when the aircraft is nearly stalled on to the ground from about 6" or less.

The approach path is normal but it does pay to have the correct threshold speed of 60 Kts., otherwise the hold-off will be prolonged as we always touch down at the same speed with a three-pointer. Notice I am using the throttle and the elevators in the conventional manner. In the flare we cannot see too well ahead, so look out to one side as on take-off, but don't be drawn to that side of the runway. During the hold-off allow the eyes to roam a bit.

You can see the threshold coming up, so looking out to the left along the runway to judge the flare — flaring now — close the throttle and hold off to the three-point attitude — stick

coming back — nose rising — to touch down on three wheels — now move the stick hard back — keep straight with prompt dabs of rudder, anticipating any swing — don't relax until the aircraft has slowed to a normal taxying speed — only apply brake with reluctance, using light stabs to avoid over-correcting. Remember that if you lock the main wheels and skid, you may nose over if the wheels suddenly grip — so be careful.

137

Now taxy back to the take-off point and complete a further circuit and landing. You have control."

STUDENT PRACTISES.

END OF EXERCISE

EXERCISE 13 — LOW-LEVEL CIRCUIT

NOTES: (1) This circuit is used when the cloudbase is low, rather than in poor visibility.

(2) The bad weather circuit is incorporated in Exercise 17B.

Aircraft Position in Flight Profile

The aircraft is about to rejoin the circuit. The instructor has control. The circuit is left hand.

Air Exercise

"Let us simulate that we have returned from a cross-country and have found that the cloudbase has lowered to 700'. We will have to carry out a low-level circuit. We call:

Springfield, Golf Papa Romeo Alpha Zulu rejoining low-level."

"Golf Alpha Zulu, you are cleared to join low-level. Runway 27 left-hand, QFE 1010."

"Golf Alpha Zulu, 27 left-hand, 1010."

Setting our normal downwind power, 2200 RPM, we join on the dead side at 500', to allow 200' separation from the cloudbase. This enables us to see other aircraft and also more of the horizon. Unlike the bad-visibility circuit, we fly this one visually. As we are joining at an unusual height, our lookout must be particularly good. Coming abeam the upwind end of the runway, turn crosswind in the normal manner, at the same time looking above to make certain that we are not being inadvertently shadowed by another aircraft. We follow the same flightpath over the ground as for a normal circuit, but, because we are low, it will appear that we are farther out. Looking behind to check our track crosswind, we wait until the tail is this side of the runway before turning downwind. This is about right, so looking right, above and to the left, make a level turn, using 30° of bank. Rolling out downwind, note that the wing tip is lying this side of the runway. We call downwind in the normal position:

Springfield, Alpha Zulu downwind, low level."

"Alpha Zulu, cleared to finals, number one."

"Alpha Zulu.

Now, you carry out the checks whilst I fly the aircraft."

139

STUDENT PRACTISES.

"Notice that the runway appears flatter and that the wing tip is still lying this side. It may appear that we are farther out, but

this is an illusion. We continue downwind to the same position as for a normal circuit. You can see that the threshold is now approximately 45° behind so, looking to the right, above and to the left, commence a level turn onto base leg, using 30° of bank. Now, rolling out as usual to allow for the drift, reduce power to 2000 RPM and, holding the height, lower half flap below 100 Kts. Adjust the power to give 80 Kts., and finally trim. We maintain level flight and 80 Kts. until we roll out after finals, when we will be on the normal glidepath. Coming up to the centreline, look right and above to clear the approach, and make a level turn, using not more than 30° of bank and add sufficient power to maintain 80 Kts. Call:

Alpha Zulu, finals."

"Alpha Zulu, you are cleared to land. Wind 260°/10 Kts."

"Alpha Zulu.

Rolling out, you should recognise the familiar picture of the runway that we see on a normal circuit. Throttling back to

1500 RPM, lower full flap and trim for 75 Kts. Now, you carry on for a normal approach and landing. You have control."

STUDENT PRACTISES.

END OF EXERCISE

EXERCISE 13 — CIRCUIT — OVERSHOOT

Aircraft Position in Flight Profile

The aircraft is on finals, at 400′ on a normal powered approach, with full flap down. The circuit is left hand.

Air Exercise

"I have control. Follow me through. I advised ATC, downwind, that we would be overshooting to help them plan the circuit traffic. We will continue the approach to 200′. Remember the briefing; if you have not been cleared to land by this height, or the runway is blocked by another aircraft, you must overshoot.

200′ coming up, so full power, check the yaw and raise the nose to hold 70 Kts. Immediately lift the drag flap to half, and raise the attitude slightly to hold 75 Kts.; retrim. Call:

> Alpha Zulu overshooting."
> "Alpha Zulu."

"Now look to the right, it's clear, so gently turn right, through about 20°, to put us on the dead side of the runway. Increasing the speed to 80 Kts., lift the remaining flap and raise the nose a bit more to hold the speed. Trim. You can now see the runway clearly, to your left, so reverse the turn to fly parallel to it. This enables us to monitor aircraft that are taking off.

142

From here, we can continue the climb to join the circuit again, but pay special attention to the position of other aircraft."

END OF EXERCISE.

EXERCISE 13 — CIRCUIT — REJOIN

Aircraft Position in Flight Profile

The aircraft is approaching the airfield at 2500' QNH at the cruise speed.

Air Exercise

"I will now show you the procedure for rejoining the circuit. I have control; sit back and watch. Well before reaching the airfield, normally more than five miles away, call up Air Traffic. Get your pencil ready to take down the airfield data:

> Springfield, Golf Papa Romeo Alpha Zulu rejoining at 2500' from the South."
> "Alpha Zulu join for runway 27 Left, Fox Echo 1009, one aircraft in the circuit and one joining from the East."
> "Alpha Zulu, runway 27 Left, Fox Echo 1009.

Now, jot down the runway and the QFE on your pad and I will carry out the field approach checks. We can use the LIFE mnemonic. Location; the airfield is five miles ahead. Instruments; synchronise the DI and set the QFE 1009. Fuel; select the fullest tank, pump on, and check the contents. Engine; check mixture rich and exercise the carb. heat. Finally, warn the passengers.

Normally we join 2000' above the airfield to examine the Signals Square. This particularly applies when you have no radio. Later I will show you the rejoin at a lower level.

We assume, if we were non-radio, that the circuit pattern is left-hand, so we arrange our heading to take us just to the right of the signals square. Keep a very good lookout and try to spot the position of the other aircraft; if in doubt, ask Air Traffic.

There is the Signals Square, so let's see what it tells us. The

letters confirm that we are at the correct airfield, and the "T" indicates the runway heading is 270°. There is no chequered arrow, so the circuit direction is left hand, and the yellow line on the red square tells us that caution must be displayed whilst landing and taxying. In future I will ask you to interpret the Signals Square.

Now, we position ourselves at 2000′ or above, on the dead side, where we let down to the circuit height of 1000′. Never descend on the live side. No-one expects it and it is therefore dangerous. To help us orientate ourselves, we can use the DI; I will show you.

Continuing the turn to the left, keep the airfield well to the inside and roll out on the runway heading 270°. We are now on the dead side and can therefore descend, so immediately select 1500 RPM, carb. air hot and commence a gentle curving

descent at 90 Kts., aiming to position ourselves crosswind over the upwind end of the runway no higher than 1000'. The purpose of the gentle curve is to look for other aircraft that could be below. It is also better to be well-established at 1000', before turning crosswind at the upwind end. In addition we can also take this opportunity to look at the windsock. You can see it near the Control Tower and indicates that we will have a slight crosswind from the right for landing. 1000' coming up, so anticipate levelling off, smoothly increase the power to 2200 RPM to hold 90 Kts. Retrim precisely. Now track at 90° across the upwind end of the runway at 1000'. Notice I am making plenty of allowance for drift. Try to locate

the position of other aircraft. If you see any coming from the right you must give way to them. Do you see that aircraft at 1 o'clock, level?"

STUDENT ANSWERS

"Well, we must slot in behind him by turning right about 20° or so, like this, so that he is about half a runway length in front when we turn downwind. Now you continue with a standard circuit. You have control."

STUDENT PRACTISES.

END OF EXERCISE.

EXERCISE 15 — ADVANCED TURNING

Aircraft Position in Flight Profile

Aircraft in cruising flight at 2300 RPM, 100 Kts. at 3000'. The instructor has control.

Air Exercise

"I will now demonstrate a steep turn to the left, follow me through. First of all, the lookout, to the left, round the front to the right, back over the top to the left, it's all clear. Rolling into the turn, increase the power to 2500 RPM. This is a 45° banked steep turn.

Note where the horizon cuts the coaming and the position of the nose from your side; it should be just above the horizon. You can see we are turning at a faster rate than a 30° bank turn. I now want you to feel the extra back pressure required. You have control."

STUDENT PRACTISES.

"I have control. Note the back pressure is quite high, and also check the visual attitude picture again before I roll out — rolling out now.

Continue to follow me through and I will demonstrate the entry and roll-out. We look out as before, left, front, right and back over the top to the left. Looking through the windscreen to watch the nose and fly the aircraft into the known attitude. Applying aileron and rudder together, at 30° of bank, add power to 2500 RPM to hold 100 Kts., and increase the back pressure with the elevators. Now check the roll with aileron, balance with rudder and here we are, once again, in a steep turn. To recover, apply right aileron with a touch of right rudder to balance, and as the bank decreases, release the back pressure on the control column and throttle back to 2300 RPM to hold 100 Kts.

I want you to practise an entry and recovery to the left and then enter a further steep turn to the left. You have control."

STUDENT PRACTISES.

"I have control. Now that we are steady in the turn, use the same sequence as with medium turns. Lookout, this is important because of the higher rate of turn. Now check the visual attitude and finally confirm it is correct inside; ball, bank, height and speed. Notice I have to use a little right rudder because of the increased power. Rolling out with aileron and rudder together, reduce the power and back pressure to hold level flight. Have you any questions?"

STUDENT ANSWERS

"Let's have a look at height control. Follow me through. Looking out as usual, roll into the turn like this, with the nose too high; we are climbing. To regain level flight, relax the back pressure to lower the nose to the correct position on the horizon. Now reapply back pressure to hold it steady. Notice I have not altered the angle of bank. Conversely, if the nose is too low — like this — we lose height. To regain level flight, increase the back pressure to raise the nose to the level attitude.

To hold the nose steady on the horizon, reduce the back pressure slightly, but still maintain the angle of bank constant with aileron. In the meantime we must not forget the sequence; lookout, ball, bank, height and speed. Rolling out — I want you to practise a steep turn to the left, initially holding your height, then vary your nose position to feel the control forces, but maintain a constant angle of bank. You have control."

STUDENT PRACTISES.

"I have control. I will now show you an alternative method of height control by varying the bank. Follow me through.

Looking out — all is clear, so rolling into the turn, but this time I will allow the bank to increase to 70° without altering the back pressure, like this. Look, the nose has dropped below the horizon and we are losing height. To regain level flight, reduce the bank like this, to about 35°, and still maintaining the same back pressure raise the nose on to the horizon. Now, to hold it there, increase the bank to the correct attitude, still maintaining the back pressure. Looking out, it's all clear, ball is central, height steady and speed 100 Kts. Rolling out — I want you to practise a steep turn to the left, adjusting your nose position with angle of bank but, at the same time, hold a constant back pressure. You have control."

STUDENT PRACTISES.

"I have control. Try not to become so engrossed in the exercise that you forget the normal checks. As with stalling and spinning, use a distinctive anchor feature to maintain your position. Carry out a LIFE check please."

STUDENT PRACTISES.

149

"I'll now demonstrate the slighty different visual attitude in a steep turn to the right, due to the side-by-side seating. Follow me through.

As before, a thorough lookout is essential; it is all clear. Rolling in with aileron and rudder, as we pass 30°, increase power and back pressure to hold the height. Check the bank here, in this attitude.

Notice that the nose spinner is below the horizon from your side, because of the offset seating. Tell me when you have the visual attitude fixed in your mind. You can then take control and continue the turn."

STUDENT ANSWERS

"You have control."

STUDENT PRACTISES.

"Now roll out — good, try another steep turn to the right and then practise turning alternatively left and right for a few minutes."

STUDENT PRACTISES.

"Fine, carry out a turn to the left, note the rate of turn visually and start to roll out when the nose passes the lake.

You can see it takes about 20° or so to roll out. Obviously, you must use that amount of anticipation to roll out on a given heading. Do a steep turn to the right and roll out pointing at the lake."

STUDENT PRACTISES.

"I have control. We'll now look at the mistakes we can make if we're careless when steep turning. Run through the HASELL checks, please."

STUDENT PRACTISES.

"Follow me through. We will enter the turn with only 2000 RPM set. First the lookout; it is all clear. Rolling to the left and increasing the back pressure, we forget to increase the power. You can see the rate of turn increasing, but the speed is decreasing. There's the horn at 75 Kts. and you can just feel the pre-stall buffet. To recover, apply full power, relax the back pressure to stop the buffet and take off a bit of bank. Now, as the speed increases, regain the correct attitude and reapply back elevator to continue with the turn. If you are solo below 3000', roll out of the turn, like this, and start again.

Did you notice the increased stalling speed?"

STUDENT ANSWERS

"At 60° of bank it is almost 50% greater than normal. Relax, while I check our position; there's the lake over to the left at 10 o'clock.

I now want you to enter a steep turn to the right with only 2000 RPM set. Then pull to the light buffet and recover as I did. You have control."

STUDENT PRACTISES.

"I have control. Follow me through. This time we'll go deeper into the stall while turning. We will still enter using a low power setting for the purpose of the demonstration. It's clear to the left, so entering the turn, increase the back pressure and once again you can see the speed washing off. There's the horn at 75 Kts. but ignoring it, continue to pull. Feel the buffet nibble, but pulling still harder — there is the heavy buffet and the aircraft is rolling — recovering — full power, stick forward — level the wings and ease out of the dive.

Did you recognise the normal standard stall recovery?"

STUDENT ANSWERS

"I want you to enter a steep turn from 80 Kts. and leave the power set at 2000 RPM. Then, tighten the turn beyond the steady note of the horn to the heavy buffet, and recover using the standard stall recovery. Remember as with any stall, you must recover if a wing drop occurs, as it did on the last recovery even though it was rolling us wings level. Sometimes, however, you will find the bank increases rapidly in the direction of the turn. You have control."

STUDENT PRACTISES.

"I have control. Although you have avoided it, I have been waiting for you to make a common mistake, and that is over-banking in the turn.

Follow me though. Looking out, enter a steep turn to the left. Increasing the bank to about 70°, you can see the attitude is wrong; the nose is below the horizon and we're losing height.

Increasing the back pressure as before, look at the nose; it remains where it was, we are still losing height and the speed is increasing rapidly; we are entering a spiral dive. To recover, close the throttle, roll the wings level with the horizon and pull to level flight.

This is potentially a dangerous situation, so, until you become more experienced, whenever you over-bank and the speed is increasing rapidly, treat it as a spiral dive and recover as I have just shown you.

As a 'rule of thumb' for height corrections, if the nose is too high, use the elevators but if it is too low, do not hesitate to reduce bank to restore the nose position.

I will now put you in some overbanked turns including a spiral dive, and I want you to recover to level flight when I hand over control. Remember to close the throttle; this is often forgotten. Have you any questions?"

STUDENT ANSWERS

"Follow me through. Looking left, it is clear, so entering the turn and over-banking — you have control."

STUDENT PRACTISES.

END OF EXERCISE.

EXERCISE 15 — ADVANCED TURNING — MAXIMUM RATE

Aircraft Position in Flight Profile

The student has satisfactorily completed steep turns at 60° of bank. The aircraft is at 3000′ at cruising speed, 100 Kts. with 2300 RPM set. The student has completed the HASELL checks.

Air Exercise

"You will remember from the briefing, I said we would look separately at the effects of speed, bank, buffet and power, on turning; then we would look at the complete turn. First, let us look at turning but without increasing the power. Follow me through.

Looking to the left, through the nose to the right and back to the left; it is all clear. Entering a turn to the left, at 30° of bank you can see a low rate of turn. Smoothly increasing the bank and back pressure to hold height, you can see the rate of turn increasing. Applying more bank and the rate of turn is even faster. You can see, therefore, that the rate of turn increases with increasing bank.

Rolling on more bank to just over 60°, increase the back pressure even more to hold our height. There is the horn at 68 Kts. — now you can just feel the buffet, watch the nose — a fraction more back pressure — the buffet becomes heavy and the nose has stopped turning — recovering to level flight.

You saw that with more bank we had a greater rate of turn but as I pulled through to the heavy buffet the rate of turn almost stopped because of the increased drag. In fact, we achieved our best rate of turn at the first signs of the buffet.

Let us check our position, we are still West of the large wood. Now, we will have a look at the effect of power on turning performance. Follow me through.

Check we are clear to the left and commence a turn. Immediately apply full power and roll to the same attitude as we had last time. You can see the speed is 90 Kts. and we have just over 60° bank. I will now increase both the bank and back pressure. Look, the rate of turn is going up — there is the horn. Now ease on to the buffet 'nibble' and hold it there. This is our maximum rate level turn with full power, we have just over 70 Kts. with about 65° of bank. The most important things to note are the attitude, the nibble on the stick, and the aircraft just on the buffet.

Rolling out now, the recovery is the same as for a steep turn, but we leave the power on to regain the cruise speed; 100 Kts., so reduce to 2300 RPM.

Now I want you to enter a maximum rate turn to the left. I will then take over and show you how to control the turn. You have control."

STUDENT PRACTISES.

"I have control. Follow me through. In the turn, keep the lookout going, which is most important because of the higher rate of turn, then check the attitude and confirm this on the instruments. Also hold the aircraft on the 'burble' like this, remember if you pull too hard, you will stop the turn.

We check our height on the altimeter, and to adjust it, we alter the nose position by varying the bank. To climb, I reduce the bank like this, whilst still holding the aircraft on the buffet. To descend, increase the bank, and maintaining the burble, wait until the correct height has been regained — now decrease the bank to hold level flight. Also, do not forget to check the slip ball as well as the altimeter. It is difficult always to fly precisely on the edge of the buffet; sometimes one can inadvertently slip though to the heavy buffet like this; to recover, relax until you find the light burble again, and now re-apply the back pressure to hold it. I will now roll out.

Practise a few turns to the left, then, when you are satisfied, try a turn to the right. The attitude to the right is similar to that in a steep turn. Any questions?"

STUDENT ANSWERS

"You have control."

155

STUDENT PRACTISES.

"I have control. Now the practical application of a maximum rate turn is collision avoidance, unless you are a fighter pilot. Which way would you turn if you see an aircraft coming directly towards you?"

STUDENT ANSWERS

"Yes, to the right, do not forget, most pilots prefer to turn left. Obviously, aviation lawyers were all sailors, not pilots. Follow me through.

Let us assume that we spot an aircraft coming straight at us. Break starboard — full aileron and power, right rudder and pull to the buffet — we are in the maximum rate turn attitude. Obviously we only need to turn to avoid the other aircraft, so we can now roll out.

You may have felt that I used considerable rudder on entry. Watch the nose and tell me which way it moves the instant I apply full right aileron. Clamp your feet on the rudder pedals. Full right aileron, now ———."

STUDENT ANSWERS

"Yes, initially it goes to the left. As with all turns you must use rudder to co-ordinate it, and the 'break' needs coarser control inputs because it is a harsh manoeuvre. Try a few breaks right and left in your own time. Momentarily establish yourself in the turn and then recover. You have control."

STUDENT PRACTISES.

"I have control. Well, that completes the exercise, but on the way back to the airfield I will call, 'Break left' or 'right'. I want you to break as soon as you can, is that clear?"

STUDENT ANSWERS

"You have control."

STUDENT PRACTISES.

END OF EXERCISE.

EXERCISE 16 — FLYING AT MINIMUM ALTITUDE

Aircraft Position in Flight Profile

Aircraft at 1500' in the low-flying area.

Air Exercise

"Before descending, check that the DI is synchronised, select the fuller fuel tank and turn the booster pump on. In addition, check that your harness is tight and that all loose articles are stowed, as it may be turbulent at low level.

Follow me through. To descend, set 1500 RPM, carb. air hot, and lower the nose to hold 100 Kts. Clear the area underneath by turning in a gentle curve or weave, like this; the airspace at low level can be quite active with helicopters and military jets. A constant lookout is very important.

Approaching 500', increase the power to 2300 RPM, select carb. air cold, and level off. Retrim. You can see that trees and buildings take on a more vertical aspect, and that the speed over the ground is much more apparent. At low altitude, the altimeter is not of much value, so you must learn to estimate the height visually; use the trees and buildings to help your depth perception. The golden rule at low level is to keep looking outside and search well ahead for hills and obstacles. If you have to look inside to check something, such as the fuel, only take a fleeting glance, and even then choose the right moment when you are straight, and flying over level ground.

Up ahead, you can see the ground is rising, so applying power early, begin a gentle climb to hold our height steady at 500'. Always anticipate the need to increase power. Even a slight gradient can make the speed 'bleed off' much more than you would imagine. Approaching the top of the hill, now reduce the power to stop the climb. Feel the extra turbulence; this can be quite heavy over hilly ground. To hold height and speed, throttle back even more as we descend. See the pylons ahead; go for the top of one, as they are easier to pick out than the wires.

Let us check the speed, so quickly glance inside and immediately outside again. 100 Kts. and steady, so increase power as the ground is levelling off again. I want you to hold this height and fly approximately on this heading. You have control."

STUDENT PRACTISES.

"I have control. Contour flying is the basis of low flying, but you must never forget the wind; its effect is more obvious than at high level. Look at that smoke at 9 o'clock, the wind is Westerly. We will follow that railway line at 11 o'clock, running in a Northerly direction, to see the effect of flying in a crosswind. Rolling out parallel to it, we are heading 350°. Watch the nose and the railway line; you can see we are drifting off to the right. In order to fly along the line, I must turn left to counter the drift, like this. Remember, when navigating at low level use wind indicators, such as smoke, to back up the forecast winds as the direction and strength can vary at low level. I will now turn left into wind. A glance inside shows that we are still maintaining 2300 RPM and 100 kts., but looking outside again at the ground, we appear to be going much slower. You are only interested in airspeed to stay flying. Remember the saying of Jim Mollison: 'Two things will get you into trouble in aeroplanes, going too quickly on the ground and too slowly in the air.'

We will now turn to the right, downwind. Looking left, to the front, to the right, it is all clear. Turning right, watch the ground on the inside; you can see we are drifting into the centre, and so guard against any temptation to relax the pull. It can be quite disorientating; better to reduce the bank until you get used to it. Now rolling out on an Easterly heading, you can see the how the groundspeed is obviously higher because of the tailwind. Obstacles approach more quickly, and you have to anticipate the use of power. Finally we will turn into wind again, by making a 180° turn to the left. Looking to the right, to the front, to the left, rolling in now. Watch the ground on the inside; you can see we are drifting out of the turn and could be in danger of hitting obstacles hidden by the wing. We must be careful, therefore, to check for hazards on the outside and anticipate by turning early. Avoid over-banking and pulling too tight, as a stall at this height could be embarrassing. I now want you to continue this pattern and practise what I have just demonstrated. You have control."

STUDENT PRACTISES.

"I have control. Now let us go to the old disused airfield over to the East. We will use the runway intersection as the centre for our turns. I will demonstrate how you have to alter the bank to arrive back over the starting point on the same heading.

Here we are, so follow me through. We will fly along the Southerly runway, which has a crosswind from the right, and then turn right up to the intersection. Here is the runway; you can see the drift. Passing the intersection, look right and roll into the turn. Initially, use only 20° of bank as we are turning into wind. As we start to face the runway downwind, gradually increase the bank to 35° to arrive over the start point again.

Now you continue with the pattern, adjusting your bank to arrive over the intersection each time. However, be cautious and remember the illusions of turning at low level. You have control."

STUDENT PRACTISES.

"I have control. We will finish the exercise with a practical application of low flying. Imagine that you have been forced down by bad weather, low cloud and poor visibility. You don't want to fly along at 100 Kts.; we can fly more slowly. Follow me through.

Reducing the speed to 80 Kts., you can see the nose is near the horizon and our forward view is restricted. Even more important, we are too close to the stall. If the weather is against us, we want to fly the aircraft as safely as possible. Setting half flap, adjust the power to hold 80 Kts., and you can see the forward view is better, the elevator and rudder feel firmer and we have increased our margin over the stall by 8 Kts. This is the configuration to use in bad weather.

In principle, fly 200' below the cloudbase in case another aircraft descends through it, and, perhaps more important, you get a better view of the horizon. Remember to monitor your speed with quick glances, and anticipate manoeuvring early. If you find the way ahead baulked, turn round early and retreat. I will raise the flap and return to the cruising speed.

I now want you to put the aircraft back into the poor visibility configuration. You have control."

STUDENT PRACTISES.

END OF EXERCISE.

EXERCISE 17A — FORCED LANDING WITHOUT POWER

NOTES: (1) The time from 2500′ AGL to the 1000′ area is approximately 2½ minutes and therefore all the patter cannot be included in one demonstration. This exercise is the standard format.

(2) Although converting speed to height is not relevant to most elementary trainers, it is applicable to many higher-speed general aviation aircraft, and therefore should be taught as a standard procedure.

Aircraft Position in Flight Profile

Aircraft in level flight at 2500′. The instructor has control.

Air Exercise

"I will now show you the full procedure for a forced landing without power; sit back and watch. Imagine we are on a cross-country flight and the engine fails — like this. Immediately, convert speed to height and trim for the glide, 80 Kts. As it is a practise, apply carb. air hot.

First choose a field and plan the circuit. If you cannot immediately see one, turn downwind. However, there is one at 9 o'clock. It is just above the left wing tip. Do you see it?"

162

STUDENT ANSWERS

"Good. The wind is from the West, so we will land in our present direction. Now select a 1000' area abeam the threshold. That copse with the greenhouse at 8 o'clock will do. It is just behind the left wing tip. Can you see it?"

STUDENT ANSWERS

"Good. It is our key position so start a gentle curve towards it, keeping the field in sight all the time. Now, and only now, check for cause of failure. F.I.C.T. — fuel on, sufficient — pump on — ignition on — carb. air hot — mixture rich — temperatures and pressures satisfactory. There doesn't appear to be anything obviously wrong that we can correct, so back to the pattern to reassess progress. We adjust our crosswind leg in order to turn downwind in the normal position, between 1600' and 1800' AGL.

Whenever you practise a forced landing, warm the engine every 1000'; otherwise you may find yourself without any power when you overshoot. I will show you. First, carb. air cold, now smoothly apply full power, raise the nose and count 'One, Two, Three'. Now close the throttle, reapply carb. air hot and resume the glide; retrim if necessary. 1600' coming up, and as we have passed over the field we can

turn downwind and carry out the crash drills; we will simulate them.

Fuel off — pump off — mixture idle cut-off — mags off — throttle closed — harness tight — canopy unlocked — warn the passengers. Leave the master switch until after full flap.

There is the copse, just in front of the nose. Check the altimeter, 1400'; we are too high, so 'dog-leg' by turning 30° right; never adjust the 1000' area.

If you have time, call 'Mayday, Mayday, Mayday, Golf Papa Romeo Alpha Zulu, PR single, two on board, engine failure, forced landing 6 miles South of Springfield.'

Now, once again, warm the engine. Carb. air cold — full power — One, Two, Three — close the throttle — carb. air hot — retrim for the glide. Here we are at the 1000' area, so turning base leg, initially aim to land one third of the way into the field.

Once we are certain of making it, lower half flap and retrim for 80 Kts. Use the base leg to adjust the glidepath; low, turn towards the field and high, turn away. Aim to turn finals at about 500' to 600'. Turning now, still maintain 80 Kts. We are certain of making the field, so lower full flap to bring the touchdown point close the the boundary and retrim for 80 Kts. Finally, turn the master switch off. Overshooting now, above 500', apply carb. air cold and full throttle, raise the nose here for 75 Kts., and immediately lift the drag flap. Trim for the climb and try to avoid flying over livestock. Finally, when we are settled, raise the remaining flap at 80 Kts.

Now climb up again to 2500' and I will show you various other aspects of the forced landing which I wasn't able to cover during this demonstration. You have control."

STUDENT PRACTISES.

END OF EXERCISE.

EXERCISE 17B — FORCED LANDING WITH POWER AND BAD-WEATHER CIRCUIT.

Aircraft Position in Flight Profile

The aircraft is in cruise flight, approaching the airfield. The instructor has control.

Air Exercise

"A forced landing with power may be required if one is compelled to land in a field because of bad weather, lack of fuel, loss of daylight hours or some other emergency. Often, it is associated with poor weather, so we will include the bad weather circuit procedure, especially as they both, sometimes, require two approaches. Sit back and watch, and I will do the flying.

Let us assume we are short of fuel, the weather is bad, with a 700' cloudbase, and it is unlikely that we can reach an active airfield. We must land as soon as possible.

Ideally, we would be looking for a grass or freshly-cut stubble field, with good approaches and sufficient length into wind. Generally speaking, it is better to turn downwind to cover the maximum distance. For convenience, however, we will assume that the aerodrome is the chosen field.

> Springfield, Golf Papa Romeo Alpha Zulu request rejoin downwind, low-level, for bad-weather circuits, over."

"Alpha Zulu, you are cleared to join downwind low-level, runway 27 left-hand, QFE 1018, over."

"Alpha Zulu, runway 27 Left-hand, QFE 1018.

First we will set the aircraft up in the best configuration for bad-weather flying. Reducing the power, check the speed is within the limits and lower half flap, like this, so that we can fly safely at 80 Kts. Notice that we require 2000 RPM and that the lower nose attitude improves the forward view.

In reality, we would also change to 121·5 and transmit a Pan call like this:

> Pan, Pan, Pan, Golf Papa Romeo Alpha Zulu, PR Single, short of fuel, attempting to land under power, about 5 miles West of Springfield.

As we are getting near the downwind leg, we will now descend to 500′ AGL to allow a safe separation from our simulated cloudbase; we will then have a better view of the horizon and also some manoeuvring space, as we don't want to pop inadvertently into cloud at low level.

Levelling off at 500′, apply 2000 RPM and trim for 80 Kts. As we are joining downwind low-level, we must be particularly careful to look out for other aircraft, as they will mostly be at the normal circuit height.

> Springfield, Alpha Zulu downwind, low-level, for overshoot."
> "Alpha Zulu, you are cleared to finals, number one."
> "Alpha Zulu.

After turning finals, we will first fly over the field at about 300′ along the most likely landing path which is approximately into wind. Our objectives are to note the drift, the heading, and the field for general acceptability, such as the approaches, overshoot area and other hazards.

Now, with the threshold about 45° behind the trailing edge of the wing, commence a continuous curve onto the final approach, using about 20° of bank. Maintain 80 Kts. all the way round with power and aim to roll out on finals at about 400′. Looking right to clear the approach, call:

> Alpha Zulu, finals for overshoot."
> "Alpha Zulu, you are cleared to overshoot."
> "Alpha Zulu.

Rolling out now, aim to fly just to the right of the intended landing path so that you can conveniently inspect the field. The landing heading appears to be 270° with a 5° drift from the left. The approaches seem good and the field is free of obvious obstructions. At the upwind boundary we will delay for 10

seconds before starting a continuous climbing turn onto the downwind leg to 500'. As a rough guide, half the windspeed represents the delay in seconds. First check for other aircraft, now rolling into a shallow climbing turn, use 20° of bank, and increase the power by approximately 300 RPM, to hold 80 Kts. We aim to roll out downwind, allowing three times the drift. As the wind will be from the right on the downwind leg, our heading will have to be 105°. Anticipating the heading, roll out now, and throttle back to 2000 RPM; trim for level flight.

> Alpha Zulu downwind low-level, for overshoot."
> "Alpha Zulu, you are cleared to finals."
> "Alpha Zulu.

Now check that we are tracking parallel with the landing run, and note landmarks that will assist us on our final circuit. That small wood at 12 o'clock is a good aiming point which will also help us judge where to start our turn. Because our nose is pointing a little way from the field to allow for drift, we must not be deceived into turning too early. This is about right now, and you can also see we are just over the wood. Looking out, apply 20° of bank and commence a continuous turn on to the final approach, still maintaining 80 Kts. Hold the speed

with power and adjust the angle of bank, within reason, to roll out on finals at 400′. Aim for a straight-in approach of about three-quarters of a mile. Looking to the right to clear the approach, you can see we will probably overshoot slightly, which means our downwind leg was too close; there must be more drift. Do not be tempted to tighten up the turn too much, but instead make a small 'dog-leg' like this.

Alpha Zulu finals, for overshoot.''
"Alpha Zulu, you are cleared to overshoot.''
"Alpha Zulu.

We now carry out a trial final approach and a low-level inspection of the field at approximately 100′, for ditches, holes and fences. Fly slightly to the right of the proposed landing path, not forgetting to maintain our speed. The surface seems good and, as we reach the upwind boundary, once again, delay for 10 seconds before turning. One, Two, Three, Four, Five, Six, Seven, Eight, Nine, Ten, turn now, using 20° of bank, and add more power to hold 80 Kts.

From the experience of our first circuit, we must increase the allowance for drift so we will roll out on a heading of 115°. Rolling out now, throttle back to 2000 RPM and retrim to hold 500′ and 80 Kts. This time we will keep the small wood just to our left; you can see it at 11 o'clock.

Alpha Zulu downwind."
"Alpha Zulu you are cleared finals."
"Alpha Zulu.

Carry out the downwind checks as usual. Brakes off — undercarriage down — mixture rich — carb. air hot — pitch fine — fuel on — pump on — flaps half — harness tight, warn the passengers — canopy unlocked and carb. air cold.

Coming up abeam the small wood, check for other aircraft and commence a turn, using 20° of bank, still maintaining 80 Kts. Once again make small bank and power adjustments to roll out on finals at 80 Kts. and 400'. Looking right to clear the approach, call:

Alpha Zulu, finals."
"Alpha Zulu, you are cleared to land, wind 260°/20 Kts."
"Alpha Zulu.

This time we are nicely lined up, so without delay, lower full flap and reduce the speed to 75 Kts. As the landing path is relatively short, aim to touch down fairly close to the boundary, which we cross slightly lower than usual at 60 Kts. Now, at about 200', reduce the speed to 60 Kts. by decreasing the power a note or two and raising the nose a fraction. At 60 Kts., reapply a small amount of power to hold the glidepath. Retrim. Only make quick glances at the airspeed. Aim to stabilise the speed and glidepath by 50'. About 100 yards to go, look outside at the boundary and touchdown point. Use power to adjust the flightpath — flaring now — stick back — throttle closed — touchdown and brake if necessary with the stick back.

As soon as possible, turn off the mags., mixture to idle cut-off, and as the aircraft comes to a stop, turn off the fuel, fuel pump, the radio and master switch, and vacate the aircraft in case of fire."

END OF EXERCISE.

EXERCISE 18 — MEDIUM LEVEL NAVIGATION

Aircraft Position in Flight Profile

Aircraft at 3000′, two miles from the base airfield, at a cruise speed of 90 Kts. The mixture has been leaned. The instructor has control.

Air Exercise

"We have climbed away from the airfield so that we can start overhead on track. Let us check the first leg; the heading is 308° with a time of 30 minutes. Make sure the stopwatch is zero, that the fuel contents are still indicating full, and synchronise the DI with the compass as accurately as possible.

As we aim to be steady on 308° by the time we leave exactly over the centre of the field, I will have to turn slightly left to intercept our heading — steady on 308°, we make a final check that the DI is synchronised.

Now, departing the field, start the stopwatch and check the actual time; it is 10 o'clock, so note this on the log and work out the ETA for the first leg. From now on make accurate flying a top priority, with particular attention to the heading and speed. In fact the most likely cause of being off track is inaccurate course-keeping.

At the start of each leg we verify that we are steering the correct course and have not misread the log or made an obvious error during the flight planning. We check this by using a suitable ground feature at the beginning of each leg. As you may remember, we highlighted this on the map during briefing. You can see that we should fly just to the right of an old railway line in a narrow valley. Looking out, we ought to be able to see it now, just to our left — Yes there it is, can you see it?"

STUDENT ANSWERS

"Good, well that confirms we are on track. We now put our map away and concentrate on lookout, and flying the heading accurately until we are within 1 or 2 minutes of our next highlighted feature, which should come up at 4 minutes. You must discipline yourself to use this technique and not to over-map-read.

We have now been flying for more than 3 minutes, so map up to check the first feature, orientate it with our heading, hold it high and read from map to ground. It shows that at 4 minutes we should fly just to the right of a small town at the end of a valley, so look ahead about 1½ miles which, as a guide, is the area just abeam the side of the engine intake.

I can see the town at 10 o'clock. Have you got it?"

STUDENT ANSWERS

"Good, we appear to be about 1 mile North of the town, and judging by this drift line we are about 4° off to the right.

Coming up abeam the town, we are on time at 4 minutes, but to regain track we must double our error which means that we have to alter course 8° to the left onto 300°. Turning left now, we will hold this heading for a further 4 minutes, when we should be back on track again.

Although it is a little early, we can take the opportunity to complete a LIFE check before we become involved in the next highlighted feature. I will do it for you this time. L — Location, we know where we are and we are keeping a good lookout. I — instruments, check the DI is synchronised, which it is; this is very important. F — fuel, check the contents and fuel consumption. E — engine, exercise the carb. heat; this should be done at least once every 10 minutes. The T.'s and P.'s are in the green and finally the mixture should be correctly leaned.

Now, once again, we put the map away until our next check feature at 7 minutes, and concentrate on the flying and lookout.

6 minutes coming up, so map up to check the next feature. At 7 minutes we should cross a road lying at 90° to our track, with a disused railway line to our right. Just beyond, there are also two small towns, separated by a small hill. Can you see them?"

STUDENT ANSWERS

"Yes, that is correct; they are over to the left as we would expect, because we are still slightly off track to the right. We will check our time over the road.

7 minutes are up and we are crossing the road, so our timing and therefore our groundspeed are good. We must wait a further minute before altering course; let's work it out. Our original heading was 308° and we found that our drift was 4° to the right. Can you tell me what our new heading should be?"

STUDENT ANSWERS

"Yes 304°, write it in your log. 8 minutes are up, so turning on to our new heading, let us cross-check the compass and DI when our wings are level — they both agree on 304°.

That is how we use the double-drift error method to regain track. Clearly it is not practical to use it beyond the halfway point on any one leg. Our next feature is at 12 minutes, so let us concentrate on the flying. You have control."

STUDENT PRACTISES.

"I have control. 10 minutes are up, so let us check the map for the next feature. You can see we have highlighted a junction of a used and disused railway line, which lies just in front of a motorway. We cross the motorway almost at right angles. Look ahead and tell me when you see the junction."

STUDENT ANSWERS

"Good, we are on track so all we need to do is to check the timing.

12 minutes are up and we are over the motorway and nicely on time. Map away and you can carry out a further LIFE check."

STUDENT PRACTISES.

173

"The next feature is interesting; it is a long hill across our track. The hill is unique as it is set in a relatively flat plain. We should cross mid-way along the hill, where the railway tunnel passes through it. Even though the hill is almost 5 minutes away, you can see it clearly, and we appear to be on track. All that remains for us to do is to again check our timing over the feature.

Nevertheless it brings up an important point. If you have such a unique feature on your planned track, once you have positively identified it and you appear to be off track, alter your heading to visually fly over it.

Passing over the hill now, the time is spot on. Also we are exactly on track, and I can make out the tunnel entrance on the right. Can you see it?"

STUDENT ANSWERS

"Good, if we now hold our heading and speed exactly, I guarantee we will reach the first turning point on track, on time, in 12 minutes. The reason is that we have definitely established our drift and groundspeed. Although it is inconceivable that the wind would suddenly increase by say 15 Kts. at 90°, if it did we would still be only just over 2½ miles off track at our turning point; from 3000′ it would in fact lie underneath the wing.

You can see from the map that the next 5 minutes of flying is over relatively featureless ground, so let us have faith in our course and steer an accurate heading. This is the secret of pilot navigation.

In the meantime you can carry out a further LIFE check. Afterwards I want you to describe the final feature which leads us into the turning point."

STUDENT PRACTISES AND ANSWERS.

"That is correct, we should pass just to the left of a large wood at 27 minutes with the town or the turning point 3 minutes further on. Also note the spot height at 830′. Tell me when you see the wood. You should be able to spot it at about 25 minutes. Meanwhile put the map away and fly the aircraft accurately. You have control."

STUDENT PRACTISES AND ANSWERS.

"Yes, I also have the wood and it is on track. I have control. Now map up to study the features of our turning point. It is a small town with a railway line leading in from the South, which is parallel to a river on the East side.

We still have about 2 minutes to go, so we can use this time to check that the compass is synchronised with the DI. Remember the technique; hold a steady course on the DI with the wings level, and take the mean reading on the compass. It shows 300°, so reset the DI on 300° and turn onto our planned heading of 304°.

Over the wood and looking well ahead you can see a town at 12 o'clock, which is probably, but not certainly, our turning point. Nevertheless, let us consider the next leg. The heading is 099°, at 3000′ and the leg time is 21 minutes. This is also a good opportunity to plan our turn on to the next course. This time I will go the long way round to ensure that we start the next leg directly overhead the turning point.

This looks like the town coming up but remember the golden rule of map-reading; 'Always make a positive identification'. Never be tempted to adjust the features on the ground to match the map; it has been done before. There are the river, railway and town all in the right order; we have made a positive identification. Do you agree?"

STUDENT ANSWERS

"As we pass overhead, first look out and now turn the long way round onto our new heading. This procedure may seem somewhat laborious but it enables us to start the new leg exactly on track. Also, it allows us time to log the ETA, 10.30, to zero the stopwatch and orientate the map for the next leg.

We aim to adjust the turn so that we roll out on heading overhead the town. 099° coming up, so rolling out on heading, start the stopwatch and check H — heading correct on 099°, and that the DI is synchronised with the compass; A — altitude, as planned at 3000' and T — time, the watch is running; log the departure time 10.33 and work out the ETA.

Can you remember the first thing we should do after setting off on a new heading?".

STUDENT ANSWERS

"Yes, that is correct; we should confirm by a ground feature that we are flying in the planned direction. On the map we can see that there is a valley going off to the left of track with a river in it and another similar valley almost along track. This latter valley leads up to our first check feature at 4 minutes, when we fly parallel to a disused railway line.

Look ahead at 12 o'clock and you can see the valley quite clearly. Our track is therefore good. Now concentrate on accurate flying until our first checkpoint at 4 minutes. You have control."

STUDENT PRACTISES.

"I have control. 3 minutes is up, so let's look for the railway. Yes, there it is to the right; clearly we have drifted left. I estimate the distance off track to be about 1 mile and we have flown about 6 miles. Using the 1 in 60 rule, that puts us 10° off track. Also, as we have 25 miles to run before the next turning point, the closing angle required is 2½°, let us say 3°; again I used the 1 in 60 rule. This means we must alter our heading 13° to the right. I will turn on to 112°.

We have made a track correction but as yet have not really made an accurate timing check. However, we are approximately correct because 4 minutes are up and you can

176

see we are now diverging from the railway line, which bends to the right.

The next 10 minutes flight time is over fairly featureless ground, so once again concentrate on accurate flying. Also we can use this opportunity to carry out a LIFE check. Notice that the fuel is unbalanced, so change tanks. However, we don't always do this, especially if the fuel is low. I will tell you more about this on the ground. Remember to put on the fuel pump and check the fuel pressure."

STUDENT PRACTISES.

"Fine, raising the map, you can see our next checkpoint is a motorway junction at 14 minutes, just to the North and ahead of a large town; we should be able to see the town 5 or 6 miles away. In the meantime put the map away and continue with the flying. You have control."

STUDENT PRACTISES.

"Can you see what looks like the town at 1 o'clock?"

STUDENT ANSWERS

"Good, I will take over control when we get a bit closer.

I have control. The time is coming up to 12 minutes, so let us use the map to remind ourselves of the features of the checkpoint. In other words we are reading from map to ground.

As we approach abeam the town, I can see the junction at 1 o'clock at about 3 miles. We will wait until we are there to check our time.

Now, opposite the junction, the watch shows 13 minutes, so we are 1 minute early. Using simple proportion, we can expect to arrive over our next turning point just under 2 minutes early, or in other words between 19 and 20 minutes on the stopwatch. Also our run-in feature point should come up at just under 17 minutes: I will amend it on the map and the ETA on the log.

I want you to fly to the turning point and identify it. On the way also point out the run-in feature. Finally go through the HAT checks for the final leg. I will then retake control and show you how to turn directly onto the next track. You have control."

STUDENT PRACTISES.

"I have control. Good, you identified that well. Over the town, we will now turn right the shortest way onto our new heading 170°. However, we will have to make a small 'dog-leg' to ensure that we start on track as we have already passed over the town. Now, passing 170°, start the stopwatch, but we must continue the turn on to about 210° to intercept our track. Holding 210° for about 20 seconds — now look behind to the right and you can see the town appearing at about 40°; we are on track and can therefore take up our correct heading, 170°.

Sometimes it is possible to identify the turning point before reaching it overhead, in which case you can turn directly onto the new heading without making a dog-leg. One can also draw the track on the map to take into account the turn.

I want you to complete the post-turn procedure and fly the final leg yourself. You have control."

STUDENT PRACTISES.

END OF EXERCISE.

EXERCISE 19 — INSTRUMENT APPRECIATION

NOTE: (1) We have used the thickness of the wing bars of the aeroplane symbol on the artificial horizon, as a criterion of attitude change, rather than the horizon line, which on modern instruments can be very narrow.

Aircraft Position in Flight Profile

Straight and level at 3000'.

Air Exercise

"I have control, sit back and watch. First we will look at the artificial horizon, the 'master control instrument' as it is sometimes called; it is the only one that gives a direct indication of bank and pitch.

Here we are in straight and level flight in the normal cruise, with 2300 RPM giving 100 Kts. Now, look at the artificial horizon. Notice that the little aeroplane symbol lies just on the lower edge of the horizon bar and parallel to it. It will help you to know, later on, that the width of the symbol bar on this model of artificial horizon represents 2° of pitch. Look outside, and you can see that the nose of the aircraft is in the familiar cruise attitude just below the horizon. Look at the artificial horizon again, whilst I ease back on the control column to move the aeroplane symbol two bar widths higher; you can now see that it lies on top of the horizon. Holding it there, look outside and notice that the nose of the aircraft has risen about 4", which on this aircraft is approximately 4°. Look inside again, whilst I raise the aeroplane symbol a further bar width. This time we have to measure by eye, as on this model there are no intermediate lines to help us. Look outside again and you can see that the nose has risen a further 2" or 2°. Easing forward on the control column, lower the symbol three bar widths to its original position on the lower edge of the horizon, and hold it there. Look outside and once again you see that the nose of the aircraft is back in the normal cruise attitude.

Now, you try the same thing, but this time start by lowering the nose. Compare it with the outside attitude. You have control."

STUDENT PRACTISES.

"Yes, that's good. Try altering the pitch only half a symbol bar width. As you can see, it requires fine control of the elevators. It is almost as if we are peering at the real horizon through the wrong end of a telescope.

I have control. In principle during instrument flying, you do not make pitch corrections of more than one symbol bar width at any one time. In fact, more often than not, one only works to half a bar width; this is equivalent to about 15 Kts. change in speed in straight and level flight, for this aircraft. I should mention that if the aeroplane symbol is adjustable, always set it to the standard position before take-off. The reason for this, as we will see later on, is that the art of instrument flying is to know the exact attitude for every phase of flight.

Now let us have a look at bank. The first small line on either side of the central point represents 10° of bank, the second line 20°, and the next, bigger one, indicates 30°.

Banking the aircraft to the left, to the 10° position like this, now look outside, and you can see the same angle of bank relative to the real horizon. Look inside again at the artificial horizon whilst I increase the bank to 30°, which is the first long line. Now look outside, and you can see the same increase in bank. Back inside, roll the aircraft to the right until the symbol is level with the horizon. Check outside, and once again we find that the aircraft's wings are level. In other words, the artificial horizon provides an immediate and direct indication of bank.

I will now roll the aircraft to the right, but this time I want you to watch the dot or small button in the centre of the aeroplane symbol, as this represents the nose of the aircraft. Here we are with 10° of bank, and the dot is lying on the bottom edge of the horizon. Holding this bank, I will now pitch the aircraft up and down like this, and you can see that the dot goes up and down relative to the artificial horizon, just as the nose, if you look outside, moves up and down relative to the real horizon. In other words, the artificial horizon gives a direct indication of pitch and bank in all attitudes up to the toppling limits if the instrument, which on this model are 60° in pitch, and 110° in bank.

I now want you to roll the aircraft to the right and left, using the artificial horizon, to a maximum of 30° of bank. Once you have established the bank, hold it and move the dot up and down to change the pitch. Normally, never use more than 30° of bank in cloud for safety reasons, and on this type of aircraft you will probably not require more than about 15° to 20°. You have control."

STUDENT PRACTISES.

"I have control. There are also relatively minor errors during acceleration and deceleration, but there are some more significant ones during prolonged turns. I will now demonstrate these. Watch the artificial horizon. Note the dot of the symbol is just below the horizon for level flight. Now, visually turning through 180° and using 30° of bank, we will roll out on 360°. Rolling out now, look at the symbol; it is about one bar width lower than it should be, and there is a small amount of residual bank. The horizon should take about 20 seconds to settle down, but remember these errors when we come to the turning exercise.

It is important to accept the fact that the artificial horizon is the only true control instrument, and for that reason it is called 'The Master Instrument'. From it radiates the scan of the performance instruments, which we will now examine.

Let us start with the DI as you are familiar with it. It is subject to precession errors, and so once every 10 minutes it should be synchronised with the compass; I will remind you how this should be done; watch me carefully.

Assuming that the DI is somewhere near the correct heading, first check that the ball is exactly central and now steer a constant course on the DI as accurately as you can, in this case, 340°. Periodically look at the compass to see what it reads; 345° seems to be the mean. You can now, at your leisure, continue to steer 340° on the DI, and when you are steady, quickly reset it to 345°, like this. Do not try to steer a straight course on the compass, as you are almost bound to induce some error, either by bank or a slight turn; this is a very common fault.

181

I want you practise synchronising the DI with the compass. I will first upset it. You have control."

STUDENT PRACTISES.

"I have control. Now, let us look at the turn-and-slip indicator. We should be well acquainted with the slip indicator, but I should like to remind you that although the wings may be level, if the ball is not central, like this, you can see the nose moving around the horizon; we are deviating from our heading. This is very often a source of inaccuracy during instrument flying.

With regard to the turn indicator, this shows rate of turn but does not provide a direct indication of bank, as some people think it does. I will demonstrate this by carrying out a visual turn, using 15° angle of bank.

Rolling in — you can now see that at this speed the turn indicator points towards the first thick line, which is a Rate 1 turn or 3° per second; this is the standard rate of turn during instrument procedures. However, still maintaining this angle of bank, if I now ease back on the control column like this, look, the turn indicator shows an increased rate of turn, although the bank is unchanged. Continuing to hold the bank constant, if I ease forward on the control column, like this, the rate of turn indicator decreases to well below Rate 1, clearly proving that it does not give a direct indication of bank. I will now roll fairly briskly to the right, and I want you to note the position of the needle immediately the wings come level with the horizon outside. Rolling level now — what did it indicate?"

STUDENT ANSWERS

"Yes, the turn indicator lags behind, especially if the roll is rapid. Remember this for future occasions.

I will now roll to the right until the turn indicator is pointing towards the second line to the right, and hold the bank visually. Rolling now — this is a Rate 2 turn. Note that the angle of bank is greater and so is the rate of turn. We very rarely use this during actual instrument flying. Levelling the wings again, I want you to roll left and right visually to find the angle of bank required for various rates of turn. Ascertain the back pressure required to maintain level flight and the relationship between the angle of bank and the movement of the turn needle. You have control."

STUDENT PRACTISES.

"I have control. I will now demonstrate errors that can occur when pulling out of a dive. Diving now, watch the turn indicator as I ease back on the stick. Initially, it remains central, but if I apply rudder, like this, the turn indicator interprets this as a large turn because of the loading. In other words, it is not reliable for keeping the wings level in the looping plane. Try that for yourself; you will probably find that you won't have to apply rudder to achieve the effect. You have control."

STUDENT PRACTISES.

"I have control. We are already familiar with the airspeed indicator and the altimeter, so let us consider the last instrument, the VSI; a useful instrument if used properly, but dangerous if abused. Its great advantage is that it provides a large angular indication for a very small rate of change of altitude. For instance, if we climb at 500′ per minute, like this, which appears as a large indication on the VSI, the altimeter needle is only moving at half the rate of the second hand on a watch.

Now, let us see what happens as I lower the nose with the control column until the VSI is indicating zero. Easing forward gently and following the VSI needle –zero coming up, so check back slightly to hold the pitch; look at the VSI needle, it goes right past until it is showing a 500' per minute rate of descent. In other words, it is very good for indicating when a change is required, but poor for making corrections because of its inherent lag. For this reason, all pitch adjustments should be made by reference to the artificial horizon.

However, if you must use the VSI to make corrections, check the pitch when the needle has moved half the distance that you require. Here we are in a 500' rate of descent, so easing back until the needle has moved half the distance to level flight, now check forward slightly and, look, the needle has settled at zero. Try using the VSI yourself. You have control."

STUDENT PRACTISES.

"I have control. With rapid changes in the looping plane or in pitch, the VSI can indicate the opposite to what is actually happening. For instance, here we are in a shallow dive. Watch the needle. Pulling fairly hard into a climb like this, the VSI momentarily shows an increased rate of descent, and even with the nose well above the horizon, it is still indicating a descent. Easing forward, the VSI is now completely out of phase, once again demonstrating that it is an instrument which has to be respected.

Finally, let us briefly have a look at how the master control instrument affects the performance instruments.

Here we are, once again, in straight and level flight at 100 Kts., with the aircraft symbol just below the horizon. Look at the VSI, altimeter and airspeed as I raise the aeroplane symbol two bar widths. Easing back now, the height increases, the speed starts to decrease and the VSI, after an initial lag, shows a climb. Holding this pitch attitude, the height still increases, but it takes some time for the speed and the VSI to stabilise. In other words, you must hold a new pitch attitude for an appreciable time before the VSI and particularly the airspeed settle.

Now, returning the aeroplane symbol to the straight and level attitude, notice the lag on the VSI, although the altimeter more or less immediately indicates a constant height. Look at the speed, it is also slow to accelerate to 100 Kts. because of the inertia of the aircraft.

This time I will lower the aeroplane symbol one bar width. Watch the performance instruments. Easing forward, the altimeter decreases, the VSI first lags and now shows a descent, and the airspeed is increasing. Holding the new attitude, the altimeter still decreases and after a time the VSI settles at 400′ rate of descent and the speed stabilises at 110 Kts. Now returning the symbol to the straight and level pitch attitude, once again the VSI lags, the altimeter shows level flight and the airspeed reduces. Holding this attitude, eventually the performance instruments settle down to the original numbers.

Now, practise making positive pitch attitude changes and then hold your attitude in order to allow the performance instruments to settle down. I will keep a good lookout. You have control."

STUDENT PRACTISES.

END OF EXERCISE.

EXERCISE 19 — PRACTICAL INSTRUMENT FLYING — FULL PANEL

Aircraft Position in Flight Profile

Straight and level flight at 3000'.

Air Exercise

"I have control. We have seen how each instrument works, and we are now going to learn how to co-ordinate them. As I mentioned in the briefing, our scan always radiates from the artificial horizon, the master control instrument, to the particular performance instruments relevant for the phase of flight. This is known as selective radial scan. In principle we only check one performance instrument before returning to the artificial horizon, but a 'trick of the trade' is to note the VSI out of the corner of your eye, when scanning the DI.

Let us begin with straight and level flight at a constant power setting. The primary performance instruments which we constantly scan are the altimeter, the VSI and the DI; the secondary instruments are the ASI and the slip indicator, which we occasionally bring into the scan.

First we check that the adjustable aeroplane symbol is in the standard position, and then select 2300 RPM which should give a cruise speed of 100 Kts. Now, from experience select the pitch attitude for straight and level flight which, for this aircraft, at this speed, is correct when the aeroplane symbol lies one bar low on the bottom edge of the horizon, like this.

To maintain a constant heading, 340°, keep the wings of the aeroplane symbol level with the horizon, and the ball central. We scan from the artificial horizon to the DI, at the same time noting the VSI out of the corner of the eye, and then back to the artificial horizon where, if necessary, we make corrections. The next time round we check the altimeter and then back to the artificial horizon. If a correction is required, for example we are now descending slightly, shown as 200' per minute on the VSI, we raise the aeroplane symbol half a bar width, hold it, retrim and remembering the new attitude, check the DI. There is no point in rechecking the VSI and altimeter immediately as the chances are we will have to lower the pitch attitude later, as it was probably a bump.

If we find that our heading has deviated, in this case 5° to the left, return to the artificial horizon and apply 5° of right bank like this, pause, level the wings and check the DI: it is correct.

As predicted, the VSI now shows that we are tending to go up, so we must lower the attitude slightly, almost to the original position. In general, the pitch attitude should approximate to the known correct one, even if occasional minor adjustments are necessary due to turbulence. As regards the sequence of scan, it is often governed by the priority of correction, but the real secret is to learn how to read the artificial horizon.

Every now and then we bring the airspeed into the scan, and of course the slip-ball which we correct immediately because it is also a control instrument. Incidentally, a small slip or skid error is often the cause of a heading deviation.

Now that we have established our heading and height, we can make small adjustments to the power to select 100 Kts. precisely. It is 103 Kts., so reducing the power a note or two, concentrate on the artificial horizon, and the VSI out of the corner of your eye, to hold level flight. Remember, however, that even the smallest power adjustment is always associated with a pitch trim change, which should be countered with the elevators.

Now I want you to practise straight and level flight at 3000' on a heading of 340°. First do it at 2300 RPM then select 100 Kts. precisely. When you have established your correct attitude, tell me what it is. I will then cover up the performance instruments to prove to you the value of attitude flying. First I will upset the trim and power setting slightly. You have control."

STUDENT PRACTISES.

"I have control. I hope you are now convinced of the value of attitude flying. To change our speed, let us say we wish to increase it to 120 Kts., scan from the artificial horizon to the RPM gauge, select the approximate power setting, 2500 RPM., and now back to the artificial horizon; check the nose-up change of trim and, as the speed increases, progressively lower the pitch attitude to maintain level flight, the VSI being a very useful instrument at this stage. Do not forget a quick glance at the ball, and then on to the DI and back to the artificial horizon to trim for our new pitch attitude.

It does help if you know the approximate pitch attitude change for any given change of speed. On this aircraft, in level flight, 20 Kts. is only equivalent to just over ½ a symbol bar width. The speed is now steady at 120 Kts. and you can see that the symbol is lying 1½ bar widths below the horizon, one ½ width lower than before.

Although the control inputs are exactly the same as for visual flight, the small indications on the artificial horizon can sometimes lead to over-controlling. The secret of instrument flying is to know your pitch attitude for every phase of flight, trim accurately whilst holding an exact attitude and to relax on the controls.

Note that we are now descending at 200′ per minute, but the speed is also 5 Kts. too high. Trading one for the other, raise the aeroplane symbol ½ a bar on the horizon and trim; the aircraft is once again flying level, and the speed is steady at 120 Kts. Note that for quite large angular deviations of the VSI needle, we need a very small pitch correction on the artificial horizon.

If you inadvertently lose 80′ or more — like this, and the speed is correct, increase the power slightly and raise the symbol a bar width, until you have regained the correct level. Now, reduce the power to the original setting and lower the symbol for normal level flight. Retrim and monitor the VSI closely for further deviations; don't, however, use it for corrections. Now, you practise reducing the speed to 100 Kts., still holding 3000′ and 340°. Remember the artificial horizon is the master instrument and that attitude flying is the key to success. Incidentally you may have noticed that, with this aircraft, a 200′ VSI deviation requires ½ a symbol bar width to correct it. You have control."

STUDENT PRACTISES.

"I have control. Now, I will demonstrate turning. During procedure flying on instruments, one normally uses a Rate 1 turn, but occasionally one may have to tighten it, such as during a 'racetrack'. However, as a matter of principle, never use more than 30° angle of bank in cloud for safety's sake. Can you remember how to calculate the angle of bank for a Rate 1 turn?"

STUDENT ANSWERS

"Yes, you add 7 to the speed in knots, excluding the last number. In this case, as we are flying at 100 Kts., we will require 17° angle of bank. Follow me through.

To turn to the left, apply left aileron with rudder to match, and concentrate initially on the artificial horizon. Check the angle of bank at 17°, like this, and maintain the pitch by keeping the centre dot of the aeroplane symbol just below the horizon, as for straight and level flight. Our primary scan includes the altimeter, VSI and DI, with a secondary scan of the turn indicator, the ASI and the ball. As in level flight, the VSI is a useful instrument to alert one of height deviations, but all corrections should be made by reference to the artificial horizon. The symbol dot is raised or lowered on the horizon with the elevators, like this. Normally restrict corrections to half a bar width, but certainly never exceed one bar at any one time. It is possible to become disorientated during turns, so concentrate, and have faith in the instruments, in particular the artificial horizon.

To roll out of the turn, anticipate the required heading by approximately half the angle of bank, let us say 10° in this case. Anticipating 180° — now, at 190°, smoothly level the wings of the artificial horizon with aileron, trying to co-ordinate the rate with the heading. It is better to roll out too early than too late, as you can always delay levelling the wings. However, remember that the artificial horizon is likely to incur slight errors after a turn, so scan the performance instruments closely. Finally, check the ball is central. Now, try a Rate 1 turn to the right onto 360°. You have control."

STUDENT PRACTISES.

"I have control. We will now practise climbing and descending; I will maintain the lookout.

To climb, we initially concentrate on the artificial horizon. Opening to full power and checking the yaw with right rudder, raise the symbol three bar widths above the horizon, and at the same time keep the wings level. This is the climbing attitude for this aircraft; hold it and trim.

Check that the ball is central and that the DI is on heading.

The scan sequence for the primary performance instruments during the climb are the airspeed and the DI; and the secondary scan are the ball and the altimeter, which we occasionally check to make certain that we do not overshoot our required altitude or miss an ATC call. As for the visual climb, don't forget the T.'s and P.'s.

We are looking for 80 Kts., but it is slightly high at 85 Kts. We must make a positive pitch attitude change by raising the aeroplane symbol half a bar width. Once again, hold the attitude and trim. Back to the DI; we have wandered 5° left. Returning to the artificial horizon, apply 5° of bank — pause — now level the wings. Check the heading — it is now correct. It may have been the ball; yes, we need a touch of right rudder. Recheck the artificial horizon for pitch and bank. The airspeed and heading are still good, so next time round bring in the altimeter, and then once again, back to the artificial horizon.

To level off at 4000', scan from the artificial horizon to the altimeter, to the DI. Anticipate by about 10% of your rate of climb, approximately 50'. 3950' coming up, so gradually lower the aeroplane symbol to the attitude for level flight, co-ordinating the pitch rate with the height. Check the DI and the ball and now back to the artificial horizon. As the speed increases, progressively lower the attitude of the aeroplane symbol to the cruise position on the lower edge of the bar, monitoring the VSI out of the corner of your eye. Now, at 100 Kts., select the cruise power of 2300 RPM and balance with

191

rudder. Rechecking the artificial horizon, hold the attitude and finally trim. Continue the scan as for level flight.

I want you to climb to 5000', level off and select the cruise for 100 Kts. You have control."

STUDENT PRACTISES.

"I have control. I will now show you descending. Imagine that we wish to go outbound on a VDF let-down, at 90 Kts., with 1500 RPM set, and on a heading of 160°. First, select 1500 RPM and now lower the aeroplane symbol two bar widths below the horizon, which we know is the approximate attitude for 90 Kts. at this power setting. Keep the wings level, the ball in the centre, check the DI for heading and then back to the artificial horizon and trim. Our primary scan includes the airspeed indicator and the DI with the altimeter being secondary, although very important. We continue to maintain our pitch attitude and the wings level with the horizon until the speed settles, and then, if necessary, make small positive pitch changes. Our speed is 95 Kts., 5 Kts. too high, so raise the aeroplane symbol half a bar width, hold it and trim. Allow the speed to settle down and in the meantime check the DI.

Note that in a descent at a constant power setting, pitch adjustments for a given change of speed are 3 times as great as in level flight. In fact half a bar width for this aircraft is equivalent to approximately 5 Kts. Continue with the scan of the DI and the airspeed, making all changes by reference to the artificial horizon. Occasionally we include the altimeter, checking it more frequently as we approach our descent level. To level off at 4000', anticipate a bit more than on the climb. Here we are with 100' to go, so smoothly raise the aeroplane symbol to the level cruise attitude at the bottom of the horizon bar. Co-ordinate the rate of pitch with the altitude, and open the throttle to 2300 RPM to increase the speed to 100 Kts. Check the ball for balance, the DI and back to the artificial horizon for minor corrections. Hold the attitude and trim, and continue the scan as for level flight.

I want you to descend to 3000' at 90 Kts., on a heading of 130° and at a power setting of 1500 RPM. You have control."

STUDENT PRACTISES.

"I have control. Now I want to show you how to descend at a constant rate. First, we will lower half flap in level flight and then descend at 80 Kts. on a constant heading of 130°, at a rate of descent of 400' per minute. At 2000', I will simulate an overshoot; this, in fact, will be a typical instrument approach profile. Holding our present pitch attitude, select 2100 RPM,

check the speed is within the limits and lower half flap; anticipate the nose-up trim change by holding our present attitude with forward pressure on the control column. Trim, and allow the speed to decrease to 80 Kts. Make small adjustments on the artificial horizon to hold level flight.

Check the ball and DI, and once again return to the artificial horizon, continuing the scan as for level flight. We are now ready to start our descent at 400' per minute. We know from experience that with 80 Kts. and half flap, we require 1700 RPM with the aeroplane symbol two bars below the horizon. Commencing the descent, throttle back to 1700 RPM with a touch of left rudder, and lower the symbol very exactly two bar widths below the horizon, hold it and trim.

Glance at the DI, and allow the aircraft to stabilise by holding the attitude on the artificial horizon.

Now check the speed, which is correct at 80 Kts., but the rate of descent is 500′ per minute, 100′ too high. To correct, increase the power a note or two, at the same time raise the symbol a fraction on the horizon, hold it and trim. Check the DI and VSI; both are good. Now back to the artificial horizon to hold the new attitude with the wings level. In the initial stage of the descent, the primary performance scan is the VSI, DI and the ASI. Check the speed; 75 Kts., 5 Kts. too low, so back to the artificial horizon, add a note of power, and lower the symbol a fraction; remember the attitude and trim. We must lead with power if the rate of descent is correct, otherwise, as with straight and level flight, the aircraft will deviate from the glidepath. Don't over-monitor the speed; you must allow it to settle. Next check the DI; we have wandered 5° right, so apply 5° of left bank — pause — level the wings and check the heading; it is good. Glance at the VSI, 450′ per minute. Leave it for a moment, it may be a bump. Back to the artificial horizon to check attitude and wings level. Glance at the altimeter, 200′ to go; from here on we will include it in our primary scan. Recheck the artificial horizon, the DI and the VSI, 450′ per minute so a glance at the speed, 84 Kts.: both too high, so back to the artificial horizon and raise the symbol a fraction; no need to use power, we have traded speed for rate-of-descent. A glance at the altimeter — 100′ to go. Our primary performance scan is now the altimeter and DI. Hold the exact attitude on the horizon. Glance at the altimeter, 60′ to go. Back to the artificial horizon. We will overshoot, so full power, right rudder and raise the aeroplane symbol two bar widths above the horizon.

All attention on the horizon; hold the attitude and wings level — trim — speed 80 Kts. Back to the artificial horizon. Ball in the centre and check the altimeter shows we are climbing. Now flaps up and simultaneously raise the aeroplane symbol one bar to maintain the speed. Trim and check the DI; we are wandering left, so back to the artificial horizon and apply slight right bank — pause — and roll wings level. Heading good, but speed slightly low, so lower the aeroplane symbol a fraction, hold and trim. Remember this attitude.

The primary performance scan during the last 150′, was the DI, VSI and the altimeter, although it is important that the speed should have stabilised by this time. During the overshoot ignore the VSI, but concentrate initially on the artificial horizon and DI, and then bring in the airspeed as the other primary instrument. I want you to climb up to 3000′ on instruments, level off and then practise a rate-of-descent and overshoot. I'll talk you through it. You have control."

STUDENT PRACTISES.

"I have control. Finally, I want to show you climbing and descending turns at 80 Kts. To climb, apply full power, right rudder to balance and raise the symbol three bar widths above the horizon, and trim. To turn left, apply 15° angle of bank and lower the symbol half a bar width to maintain the speed. Our scan is the artificial horizon and airspeed, bringing in the DI and altimeter, according to importance. The angle of bank for a Rate 1 turn is slightly less than in level flight because of the lower speed, but the rate of turn should occasionally be checked.

To descend in the turn, concentrate mostly on the artificial horizon; so throttling back to 1500 RPM, maintain the angle of bank, but gradually lower the dot of the symbol to a shade below the normal descent attitude, hold it and trim. The performance scan embraces the airspeed, the DI and altimeter, according to importance. To level off and stop the turn, level the wings on the artificial horizon and raise the symbol dot to the cruise attitude, simultaneously applying cruise power of 2300 RPM. From here on, scan as in level flight.

Now try a climbing turn to the right, and once you have held it for a short time, commence a descending turn in the same direction, holding the speed constant with the elevators and the power at 1500 RPM. You have control."

STUDENT PRACTISES.

END OF EXERCISE.

EXERCISE 19 — PRACTICAL INSTRUMENT FLYING — LIMITED PANEL

Aircraft Position in Flight Profile

Aircraft cruising at 3000'.

Air Exercise

"I have control. We will assume that we have lost the vacuum and therefore the DI, and more important the artificial horizon. I will therefore cover these instruments up. The technique is very different from full panel, as we have no direct indication of pitch or bank. To a large extent, use feel and experience.

Follow me through on the controls. First of all, level flight. The VSI is the only instrument that can anticipate the altimeter. Let us see how we use it. Here we are in level flight at 3000'. The VSI starts to go up. To correct, ease forward until the needle has returned halfway to the zero and then check back slightly. The needle hesitates slightly and then returns to the zero. We are once again back in level flight. Similarly, if we start to descend slightly, like this, ease back on the control column until the VSI needle has moved half the distance to the zero and then check slightly forward; the needle returns to zero. The VSI possesses inherent lag and you have to take this into account. Obviously the altimeter is the primary instrument for level flight, and if we deviate markedly we have to use it as our criterion. Now try using the VSI and the altimeter to maintain level flight. You have control."

STUDENT PRACTISES.

"I have control. To maintain a constant heading, use the turn indicator as an indirect indication of bank. Keep it central with aileron. If it oscillates an equal amount both sides of centre, do not attempt to correct: if it is obviously to one side, correct with aileron, but there is a lag. I will show you. Look outside and compare the indication of the turn needle when the wings are level. Levelling the wings now, what did you see?"

STUDENT ANSWERS

197

"Yes, the technique is to centralise the ailerons when the needle has moved half the deflection required. Now try maintaining the wings level with the turn needle. You have control."

STUDENT PRACTISES.

"I have control. We will utilise this technique to maintain a particular heading. First, let's consider Easterly and Westerly headings. Here we are on 090°. Momentarily banking the aircraft like this, without changing direction, the compass reads constant. Obviously there are no bank errors on East. The same applies to West.

I will now turn on to 360°. On Northerly headings, if you momentarily bank the aircraft, like this, the compass shows a turn in the opposite direction. Level the wings again, and the compass returns to the original heading. On Southerly headings, the opposite happens. If, however, after levelling the wings on Northerly and Southerly headings, you notice that you have obviously deviated, divide the error by three and turn in the appropriate direction for that number of seconds. I will show you. Here we are 9° to the right of North; we must turn for 3 seconds to the left, so rolling in, count, one-thousand-and-one, one-thousand-and-two, one-thousand-and-three; now roll level and wait for the compass to settle down. There we are on North. Now I want you to try to maintain a constant heading, if necessary making corrections, and then combine it with level flight. You have control."

STUDENT PRACTISES.

"I have control. Follow me through. Now, I will show you climbing. First the lookout, level and above — all is clear. Applying full power and right rudder, gently ease back on the control column and simultaneously keep the turn needle central with aileron. We are looking for 80 Kts., so 10 Kts.

before, check forward slightly, hold by feel and trim. Wait for the speed to settle — 84 Kts. It is still slightly high, so ease back again and check at half the error to be corrected. Wait for the speed to settle — 80 Kts. Every time you have to make a correction, check before the speed has reached the required figure. Now try adjusting the speed in the climb yourself. You have control."

STUDENT PRACTISES.

"I have control. I will show you how to level off at 4000'. Now, 50' before, ease forward on the control column until the VSI needle has decreased half-way to zero, in this case 250' per minute. Now check back very slightly, hold and trim, and throttle back to 2300 RPM just as the speed reaches 100 Kts. As in normal level flight, make final adjustments to the airspeed, height and direction.

I want you to climb to 5000' and level off. You have control."

STUDENT PRACTISES.

"I have control. Follow me through. I will now show you a descent to 4000'. Never make an abrupt entry on limited panel, as you might find yourself inadvertently in a spiral dive. We are looking for 90 Kts., so close the throttle smoothly to 1800 RPM and allow the nose to drop by feel. 10 Kts. before, check with slight up elevator, hold and trim. Wait for the speed to settle down, and then make speed corrections as you do for the climb. The speed is slightly high at 96 Kts., so raise the nose with back pressure until it is 93 Kts. — now check, trim, and once again allow the speed to settle. There it is at 90 Kts.

To level off, anticipate by 100'. 4100' coming up, so ease gently back on the control column, keeping the wings level by reference to the turn needle. When the VSI needle is half the original rate of descent as it is now, check forward slightly, hold and trim, and apply cruise power of 2300 RPM. Check the balance with rudder, and make final adjustments to height, speed and direction. Now try a descent to level off at 3000′. You have control."

STUDENT PRACTISES.

"I have control. Follow me through. I will now show you turns. Never use more than a Rate 1 turn on limited panel; keep your angle of bank to a minimum. In order to turn to the left, very smoothly apply left bank with aileron, a touch of left rudder and watch the VSI like a hawk, for tendencies but not for corrections. Apply a small amount of back pressure on the elevators and, just before the turn needle indicates Rate 1, check the roll with aileron. During the turn, hold the control column lightly with the ailerons constant, and allow the natural stability of the aircraft to maintain the angle of bank.

The VSI is now showing a slight descent, so correct with a fractional increase in back pressure on the elevator, ignoring the turn indicator which increases very slightly. Once the descent has been checked and the altimeter is steady, relax very slightly and continue with the turn. Notice the turn needle once more shows a Rate 1. Only reduce the angle of bank if you are positive the rate of turn has increased. In other words when you are making pitch corrections, do not take too much notice notice of the turn needle.

The altimeter is steady and the VSI is zero. The turn needle, however, shows a slight increase in rate of turn, which means too much bank as our height is constant. To correct, reduce the bank very slightly with aileron and relax fractionally on the elevators. The VSI remains at zero, and we continue with the turn. To stop the turn, apply right aileron with a touch of right rudder, until the turn needle is not quite central — now centralise the ailerons and relax the back pressure. Continue the scan as for straight and level flight. Try some Rate 1 turns, left and right. You have control."

STUDENT PRACTISES.

END OF EXERCISE.

EXERCISE 19 — PRACTICAL INSTRUMENT FLYING — COMPASS TURNS

Aircraft Position in Flight Profile

Straight and level at 3000′.

Air Exercise

"I have control. I will now demonstrate compass errors, whilst turning at Rate 1 through 360°. Sit back and watch.

Starting from North, we will turn right and compare the headings on the DI with those of the compass. Rolling right now, immediately the compass indicates a turn in the opposite direction of about 30°; it retains this error for a short while, but now, as we pass through 030° on the DI, it is lagging slightly less than before. As we approach East, the compass starts to catch up until finally it reads correctly as we pass 090°. Turning through 120° on the DI, the compass starts to over-read, until on South you can see it is indicating 210° or over-reading by 30°. Continuing the turn through 230°, the compass starts to slow down until we pass West, when it reads correctly. Continuing towards the North, the compass starts to lag again. As we approach 360° on the DI, the compass still only reads 330° or a lag of 30°. Rolling level now, the compass catches up and finally reads 360° as the wings become level. I hope this adequately demonstrates what I briefed on the ground.

Now let us carry out a turn to the right onto a specific heading, 050°, with the DI covered. We know that the compass will under-read and that the error will be approximately half the maximum, or in other words 15°. Commencing the turn, we must anticipate by rolling out when the compass reads 035°. Rolling the wings level now, look — the compass catches up, almost onto 050°; 053° to be precise. To make the final adjustment, turn left for one second — now roll the wings level and there we are, on a heading of 050°.

Let us continue the turn onto 180°. Rolling in, we know the compass will over-read by a maximum of 30° on South. We will therefore roll out when it reads 210° — 210° coming up, so smoothly levelling the wings, and look — the compass reverses onto 180°.

201

In a nutshell, if you turn on to Northerly headings, you roll out early, and on to Southerly headings, you roll out late, allowing a maximum of 30° in each case. On East and West, the compass reads correctly, and on intermediary headings, the amount you allow depends on how close you are to North or South.

Keeping the DI covered, I want you to turn onto various headings, using the compass. Use a Rate 1 turn and fly smoothly. You have control."

STUDENT PRACTISES.

"I have control. Finally, I will demonstrate acceleration errors which only apply on Easterly and Westerly headings. We will use the DI. Here we are on 090°, with 1800 RPM set. Opening to full power and increasing the speed, look — the compass is indicating a turn towards North. Now closing the throttle, the speed decreases, and look — the compass indicates a turn towards the South. I will not ask you to practise this, but remember it when flying faster aircraft. The same errors apply on Westerly headings.

Finally on East and West there are errors during the climb and descent. Steady on 090°, we enter the climb. Now look at the compass, it indicates 085°. Throttling back to descend, look again at the compass, it indicates 095°. Lesson learnt, do not synchronise your DI whilst climbing or descending. Have you any questions?"

STUDENT ANSWERS

END OF EXERCISE.

EXERCISE 19 — PRACTICAL INSTRUMENT FLYING — TIMED TURNS.

Aircraft Position in Flight Profile

Aircraft in normal cruise at 3000'. The instructor has control.

Air Exercise

"Assuming that we have lost our DI, I will now show you timed turns, which have the merit that you don't have to take compass turning errors into account. We always turn at Rate one, the first division on the turn indicator, or, in other words, 3° per second. We use the artificial horizon to help us, and you may remember that we can calculate our angle of bank by adding 7 to the first two numbers of the speed. In this case, 100 Kts. plus 7 equals 17°. Always start from wings level and make sure you are in unaccelerated flight. To turn from this heading, 090°, to 270°, will take one minute. Follow me through.

Starting the watch, simultaneously roll smoothly into the turn — stop the bank at 17° on the artificial horizon. Now check the turn indicator, and if necessary make small bank adjustments on the artificial horizon, but it seems correct. Don't forget the remaining scan — ball, altimeter, pitch and bank.

We commence to roll out when exactly one minute is up. This allows for the lag when we started. Checking the watch, it is just coming up to one minute — now roll out smoothly, hold the wings level and wait for the compass to settle down. Not bad, 265°, but we must turn right for two seconds; we will count them. Rolling in, one-thousand-and-one, one-thousand-and-two, now level the wings. Wait for the compass to settle. There it is, exactly on 270°.

I want you to turn left on to 180°, timing your turn. Tell me what you are doing. You have control."

STUDENT PRACTISES.

END OF EXERCISE.

EXERCISE 19 — PRACTICAL INSTRUMENT FLYING — UNUSUAL POSITIONS (PART I)

NOTE: (1) It is appreciated that it is probably better to use the altimeter, if it is modern, in preference to the ASI, for pitch level assessment.

Aircraft Position in Flight Profile

Aircraft in normal cruise at 4000'. HASELL checks completed.

Air Exercise

"Before we start this exercise, I want to emphasise that if your artificial horizon is still erect and you have no reason to doubt its serviceability, use it to try to regain level flight. However, if it has toppled, or the vacuum pump has failed, then you must use the turn-and-slip and the other performance instruments to regain level flight. The only exception is the VSI, which can be very misleading. I will cover up the artificial horizon. I want you to compare the instrument indications to the actual visual attitude. First, let's start with climbing and descending and how to regain level flight.

Follow me through. Putting the aircraft into a gentle dive, you can see the speed increasing from 100 Kts. and the altimeter shows we are losing height. To regain level flight, ease back on the elevators and watch the ASI. It's stopped increasing, so centralise the control column and transfer to the altimeter to establish level flight. Look outside, and you can see we are in the level attitude. As soon as the ASI reverses its trend you are just about level. Then go onto the altimeter.

Now, putting the aircraft into a gentle climb, you can see the speed is decreasing. To recover, ease forward on the control column until the speed has stopped decreasing, now check back slightly and transfer to the altimeter for fine adjustments. Looking outside, we are back in the level attitude again. Notice I did not demonstrate extreme attitudes, and therefore did not have to use power.

204

Let us now look at a recovery from a steep dive. Easing forward with the elevators, you can see the speed is increasing rapidly through 120 Kts. To recover, close the throttle and ease back on the control column. Watch the speed, it has stopped increasing, so check slightly forward on the control column and transfer to the altimeter. Check the speed; it is reducing to 100 Kts., so open the power to 2300 RPM and make small adjustments for level flight. Have you any questions?"

STUDENT ANSWERS

"Good, finally I'll put the aircraft into a steep climb. Easing back on the control column, look, the speed is decreasing quickly. To recover, apply full power and ease the stick forward until the speed has stopped decreasing — now check slightly back on the control column and transfer to the altimeter to maintain level flight. Check the speed; it is coming up to 100 Kts., so throttle back to 2300 RPM and once again we are in the normal cruise. Notice that I did not once refer to the VSI. Never be persuaded to use it during unusual positions.

I now want you to practise for yourself how to regain level flight. Start by visually putting the aircraft into a gentle climb or dive. Then recover to level flight on the instruments, but at the same time relate the visual attitude with the instrument indications. This should give you confidence. You have control."

STUDENT PRACTISES.

"I have control. The other main instrument is the turn needle, which we use to level the wings. Remember though, it only gives an indirect indication of bank, and I will now demonstrate why you have to be careful when using it. Rolling into a 30° banked descending turn, watch the turn needle. At the moment it shows just over Rate 1, but if I pull back on the control column like this, look, the rate of turn has increased even though the bank has not changed. Conversely, easing forward on the control column, look, the rate of turn decreases. I will roll back to wings level. The rate of turn indicator is subject to errors under 'G'. With positive 'G' it will over-read, and with less than 1 'G' it will under-read. Therefore, before using the turn needle to level the wings, you must first remove the 'G'.

I will now show you the lag inherent with the turn indicator when levelling the wings. Follow me through. Here we are in a 30° banked turn. The turn needle is indicating Rate 2. When I roll out, I want you to note the position of the turn indicator when the wings become level. Rolling out now — what did you see?"

STUDENT ANSWERS

"Yes, when the wings became level, the turn needle had only returned halfway to the centre. Lesson learned, you have to take this into account when checking the roll. Now you practise this to satisfy yourself. You have control."

STUDENT PRACTISES.

"I have control. In practise the most critical unusual positions are the steep descending or climbing turns. I said in the briefing that you must try to ignore your senses, but instead conform to a drill. First, you assess the situation from the instruments, then you carry out the recovery 'according to the book'.

First, we will consider the spiral dive situation. Watch the instruments. Follow me through. Putting the aircraft into a diving turn to the left, the instruments confirm this as the speed is increasing and the turn needle is over the left. To recover — close the throttle — relax the 'G' — roll until the turn needle is half its deflection — check it is central and pull, with ailerons neutral until the speed starts to reverse — now check slightly forward, transfer to the altimeter and set cruise power when the speed has reduced to 100 Kts. Finally trim.

Note that when I pulled into level flight, I ignored the turn needle, because under load the turn indicator will interpret the slightest yaw as a high rate of turn.

I will put the aircraft into a few spirals and, using this technique, I want you to regain straight and level, after I give you control. Watch the instruments. Follow me through. You have control, recover now."

STUDENT PRACTISES.

"I have control. Finally, we will have a look at the steep climbing turn, in this case to the left. Watch the instruments. Looking out to the left and above, it's clear, so putting the aircraft into a climbing turn, you can see the speed is decreasing and the turn needle is over to the left. To recover — apply full power — relax the 'G' — roll until the turn needle is half deflection — now check it is central and ease gently forward until the speed starts to increase — now check slightly back — watch the altimeter and allow the speed to build up to 100 Kts. Finally select cruise power and trim. Have you any questions?"

STUDENT ANSWERS

"Good, watch the instruments while I put the aircraft into a few climbing turns and recover when I hand over control. Follow me through — you have control, recover now."

STUDENT PRACTISES.

"That is the end of the exercise on the recovery from basic unusual positions. The secret is to ignore your senses, keep cool and work to a drill. However, let us hope you never get into any of these situations 'for real'. On the next flight, we complete the exercise by covering the stall and spin recovery action on instruments."

END OF EXERCISE.

EXERCISE 19 — PRACTICAL INSTRUMENT FLYING — UNUSUAL POSITIONS PART II

NOTE: (1) Where appropriate, only aircraft cleared for the recovery from the vertical should be used.

Aircraft Position in Flight Profile

Aircraft in normal cruise at 4000′. The student has revised the recovery action from basic unusual positions.

Air Exercise

"We will now cover the instrument recovery from the stall and the spin. First I want you to carry out the HASELL checks."

STUDENT PRACTISES.

"I have control. First we will have a look at the stall and recovery on full panel. Follow me through.

Turning to lookout; it all seems clear. Throttling back to idle and holding the height, look, the speed is decreasing and the aircraft symbol is higher on the artificial horizon. There is the warning horn at 64 Kts. and clearly we should recover now, but we will go further into the stall. Speed decreasing through 60 Kts., with a little buffet and at 56 Kts. recover — full power — stick forward to lower the nose on the artificial horizon — a touch of right rudder and you can now see the aircraft symbol about 5° below the horizon. As the speed builds up to 70 Kts. we can ease out of the dive until the symbol is in the normal climb attitude. Look at the delay in the altimeter reading even though we are in the climb.

Throttling back for the normal cruise, I want you to go onto instruments; I will talk you through the lookout turns and then you can try a stall and recovery on instruments. You have control."

STUDENT PRACTISES.

208

"I have control. Relax, while I carry out a further lookout and then we will try a limited panel stall and recovery. Cover the horizon for me, please.

Rolling out and slowly bring the throttle to idle. Watch the instruments. Keep the wings level with the turn indicator and maintain the height by gradually easing back on the control column. We have to use 'feel'. We will recover at the buffet. There is the horn and now the buffet — recovering — ease centrally forward on the control column and full power — check turn needle and ball central — buffet stopped and speed increasing to 70 Kts., so ease back on control column until the speed is steady — now throttle back and continue as for level flight.

Later on we will also have a look at recoveries near the stall in banked attitudes. However, as I said in the very early stalling exercises, we must not ignore the warning horn.

I will put the aircraft into some approaches to the stall, initially with the wings level. I want you to recover as soon as the horn gives a steady note. Watch the instruments whilst I carry out a clearing turn. Follow me through — approaching the stall — you have control — recover now."

STUDENT PRACTISES.

"I have control. Let us now have a look at the two extreme cases I mentioned in the briefing. As we will be close to a spin, we should therefore be above 5000'. I want you mainly to watch the instruments and only glance at the real horizon to confirm the indications. Follow me through.

Looking out in a steep turn and diving to increase the speed, here we are at 120 Kts. Now pulling up into a steep climbing turn to the right — the speed is 60 Kts. decreasing; the turn indicator is over to the right; we must recover from the vertical — clamp the control column and rudder pedals firmly and wait. Look, the speed has stopped decreasing; we are nosing over; it can be quite violent — speed now building up above 70 Kts., so throttle to idle, check you are not pulling, and roll the wings level on the turn indicator— there is the half deflection, so centralise the ailerons and ease out of the dive as in a normal spiral recovery.

It is unlikely that you will enter a spin when recovering from an unusual position that has started initially from a steep near vertical attitude. More likely you will be in a spiral dive.

Watch the instruments as I put the aircraft into a few similar attitudes. I will tell you when to recover. Follow me through — you have control, recover now."

STUDENT PRACTISES.

"I have control. We will finish the exercise by having a look at the instruments in a spin and during the recovery, especially the turn needle and ASI. Follow me through and watch the instruments. Carrying out a 360° turn for a thorough look out; it is all clear below. Rolling the wings level, bring the power to idle. Speed decreasing — 60 Kts., full rudder and control column fully back with ailerons neutral. Here we are in the spin, look, the ASI is settling down at 40 Kts. and not increasing. Most important the turn needle is hard over to the left. Recovering — full right rudder and ease the stick centrally forward — watch the turn needle — there it flicks across — firmly centralise the rudder and control column — check that the speed is increasing and we can now recover from the ensuing spiral as before.

I want you to climb up again to 6000', update the HELL checks, and carry out a spin. As in the earlier demonstrations watch the instrument indications and back them up with the visual attitude. Remember, the purpose of this exercise is to hammer home the difference between a spiral dive with speed increasing, and a spin with a steady speed indicated. You have control."

STUDENT PRACTISES.

END OF EXERCISE.

EXERCISE 19 — PRACTICAL INSTRUMENT FLYING — STEEP TURNS

Aircraft Position in Flight Profile

Aircraft in cruise at 4000'.

Air Exercise

"Today, as we discussed on the ground, we will have a look at full panel steep turns. This requires precise flying with the artificial horizon, although obviously it should be backed up with radial scan. I want you to watch the instruments whilst I maintain the necessary lookout during the turn. Follow me through.

We are level at 4000' at 100 Kts., and you can also see on the artificial horizon that the aircraft symbol is level just below the horizon bar. Looking left, it all seems clear, so rolling smoothly into the turn with aileron and rudder, keep the button of the symbol level on the bottom of the horizon with elevator, but do not trim. At 30° of bank, add power to about 2500 RPM to maintain the speed, and simultaneously increase elevator back pressure to hold the button just below the horizon bar. At 45° of bank, check the roll with aileron and to maintain the turn, hold the bank angle steady and the button below the bar. Now, scan the altimeter and VSI to check for level flight, and back to the horizon again to make sure the attitude is still steady. Also include, from time to time, the slip-ball and the airspeed, adjusting the rudder and power if necessary.

As for visual steep turns, anticipate rolling out by about 30°. I will roll out on South, so waiting for 210° to come up, level the wings now, simultaneously reducing the power to 2300 RPM and relaxing the back pressure to hold the button on the bottom of the bar. Scan the VSI and altimeter, and make precise pitch adjustments on the artificial horizon. Finally, make small heading corrections with aileron.

Have you any questions?"

STUDENT ANSWERS

"I will now show you how to correct for height and VSI deviations. Remember that the artificial horizon is subject to bank and pitch errors in turns, especially when they are steep. From time to time, therefore, you will inevitably have to make positive attitude adjustments to hold the height. Follow me through.

Still continue to watch the instruments; I will maintain the lookout. Re-establishing the turn, scan the VSI out of the corner of your eye. Whenever it deviates 200′ per minute, adjust the button of the symbol half a bar width by squeezing and relaxing the back pressure, like this.

If the VSI deviations are greater, up to 500′ per minute — you can see we are now descending at 400′ per minute — raise the button symbol one bar width like this, hold it, and maintaining the bank, wait for the VSI to settle down. If necessary make small adjustments to the pitch attitude to bring the VSI to zero.

If our descent is more than 500′ per minute — like this — reduce the angle of bank to 30° — raise the button one bar width — wait until the VSI is halfway to zero — now reapply 45° of bank and adjust the back pressure to hold the button just below the horizon. Finally, recheck the bank and make small adjustments to the attitude to hold the VSI level.

It is unlikely that you will get large deviations of ascent, but if you do, do not exceed 45° of bank during corrections.

I now want you to practise steep turns and I will give you headings on which to roll out. Tell me which way you are going, so I can look out first. You have control."

STUDENT PRACTISES.

END OF EXERCISE.

EXERCISE 19 — PRACTICAL INSTRUMENT FLYING — TAKE-OFF

NOTE: (1) It is assumed that artificial horizon acceleration errors are very small and can therefore be ignored.

Aircraft Position in Flight Profile

The aircraft at take-off point. Checks complete.

Air Exercise

"I will now demonstrate an instrument take-off, so sit back and watch. Let us assume that the visibility is about 200 yards, and that the cloudbase is practically on the surface. We will therefore have to transfer to instruments during rotation. We call:

> Springfield, Golf Apha Zulu ready for departure."
> "Golf Alpha Zulu, cleared to take-off. Wind light and variable."
> "Golf Alpha Zulu.

As we cannot see anybody on the approach, it is in our best interests, if in doubt, to double-check on the radio that all is clear. Now taxy slowly onto the centreline, to avoid artificial horizon errors. Roll forward a few yards to straighten the nosewheel, and apply the brakes. Before rolling, confirm with the DI that we are on the correct runway, the artificial horizon is erect and that our nav. aids are set and functioning. Now open up on the brakes to 2100 RPM, 75% power; check T.'s and P.'s and call:

Golf Alpha Zulu, rolling.

Heels on the floor, release the brakes and open to full power, keeping straight with rudder on the centreline. Check 2300 RPM and speed increasing. We transfer to the artificial horizon at 55 Kts., 5 Kts. below rotation. 55 Kts. coming up, so concentrate on the artificial horizon. 60 Kts., rotating smoothly to raise the symbol two bar widths and keep the wings level. Maintain this climbing attitude until the altimeter

213

indicates 50′. Now start the scan; speed, DI, horizon, ball, speed, horizon, and continue with the climb on instruments. You have control."

STUDENT PRACTISES.

END OF EXERCISE.

EXERCISE 20 — NIGHT FLYING

Aircraft Position in Flight Profile

Aircraft on the apron with the engine running. Taxy clearance has been given for runway 27 left.

Air Exercise

"I have control. We will follow the taxy lights to the take-off point, but we must be careful with our lookout until our eyes become accustomed to the dark. We taxy in the centre of the two rows of blue lights. Look ahead for other aircraft. They are difficult to see from behind, as only their tail and anti-collision lights are visible. If in doubt, use your landing light, or even stop. Don't hesitate to ask Air Traffic. It also helps if you can build up a picture, from radio calls, of the position of other aircraft on the ground. Beware of taxying too fast. Look out to the side and note the rate at which the lights go past; it may surprise you. Now continue to taxy to the marshalling point, and I will tell you how to identify it. You have control."

STUDENT PRACTISES.

"If you look ahead you should see a lighted board with 'H' on it. That is the marshalling point, but we must double-check that it is for the correct runway. You can now see the number '27' on it. Approach slowly, as there may be other aircraft running up. Now turn into wind and carry out your normal engine and pre-take-off checks, but be particularly careful that your brakes are holding."

STUDENT PRACTISES.

"I have control. As our eyes become accustomed to the darkness, the cockpit lighting seems brighter, so we will lower its level slightly to help our night vision.

215

I will now show you a normal take-off; there is no need to follow me through. I want you to take particular note of the pattern of the lights when we line up, as that is how they will appear when you land. Also, note the attitude after we rotate. First, we will taxy forward and stop at the holding point so that we can see aircraft on the final approach.

"Springfield, Alpha Zulu ready for departure."
"Alpha Zulu, clear to take-off. Wind 260°/10 Kts."
"Alpha Zulu.

Now check for aircraft on the approach. One is still obliged to do this, despite clearance for take-off. Often aircraft put their landing lights on to help Air Traffic. It all seems clear. Moving on to the runway, I will pause on the centreline so that you can memorise the light pattern for landing. Now look at the lights at the far end of the runway, and, as in daytime, smoothly open to full power, keeping straight with rudder.

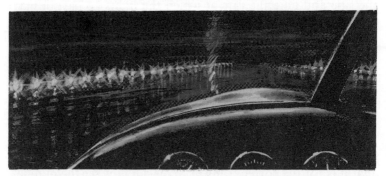

Check full power, 2300 RPM, and speed increasing. We will rotate at 60 Kts.; note the attitude. Rotating now — nose on horizon and hold it until the runway lights vanish. Airborne,

so transfer to instruments, hold a 5° climb attitude on the artificial horizon, and check the speed is 80 Kts. Beware of lowering the nose too much to hold the speed; not more than half a bar width at a time. Passing 200', so raise the flap and continue the climb straight ahead at 80 Kts.

Although I am flying on instruments, there is clearly sufficient reference from lights outside to fly visually. Nevertheless, always make the initial climb on instruments. We will clear the circuit so that you can have a look at the airfield and the lights of the town and villages:

Springfield, Alpha Zulu climbing straight ahead to clear the circuit. We will operate at 2000'."
"Alpha Zulu, call rejoining."
"Alpha Zulu.

You can probably recognise Springfield town at 11 o'clock. But remember, after 12 o'clock when the lights go out, towns can change their shape. In modern times we mostly use radio aids to navigate at night. The main point to note is how we use a blend of visual and instrument flying at night. This will depend on the conditions, whether it is very dark, or if there is a moon. However, you must still look out for other aircraft and remember the lights that stay on a steady bearing are the ones to avoid. Fly the aircraft around for a few minutes. When you are ready, we will return to the circuit. You have control."

STUDENT PRACTISES.

"I have control. We call up to rejoin in the same manner as in daylight:

Springfield, Golf Papa Romeo Alpha Zulu rejoining from the South at 2000', over."
"Alpha Zulu, cleared to join runway 27 left hand, QFE 1012."
"Alpha Zulu, 27 left hand, QFE 1012.

Field approach checks are normal. Set the QFE 1012 — synchronise the DI — fuel sufficient on the fullest tank — pump on — mixture rich — engine T.'s and P.'s in the green — and exercise the carb. air control.

217

First, we will fly overhead at 2000′ to have a look at the airfield layout. Also, try to picture the position of other aircraft in the circuit from the radio calls. If in doubt, call Air Traffic. You can recognise the beacon flashing the airfield identification in Morse, and you can also see the runway lights quite easily. However, people have mistaken street lights for the flarepath, so always make a habit of positively identifying the runway.

We will now join the normal traffic pattern and I will demonstrate how the flarepath appears on the final approach. Let down on the 'dead' side in the normal manner to 1000′. We do it in a gentle curve like this, to help our lookout. Judging from the radio calls, there is one aircraft downwind and another just about to touch down. We must not, however, ignore the possibility of an aircraft with a radio failure, so keep a good look out. Tell me if you see another aircraft.

1000′ coming up, so power up to 2200 RPM and trim for level flight. We turn crosswind in the normal position, over the upwind end of the runway, and wait for the tail to cross abeam the flarepath. Now look right, over the front, to the left, and turn downwind. Glance at the artificial horizion to check the bank and I will use the DI to help me roll out on the correct heading. You can see the flarepath, so rolling out parallel to it, check the DI is 090°, and the wing tip is running down the lights. It is important that we make accurate position calls to help Air Traffic and other aircraft to locate us:

> Alpha Zulu downwind, flarepath demo."
> "Alpha Zulu, cleared to finals number two."
> "Alpha Zulu.

As usual, carry out the downwind checks: brakes off — undercarriage down — mixture rich — carb. air hot — pitch fine — fuel pump on, and contents sufficient for overshoot — flaps up — harness tight — canopy closed — carb. air cold. Can you see the end of the flarepath?"

STUDENT ANSWERS

"For this demonstration we will go farther downwind than the normal 45° position. I will use the DI to help maintain the correct heading. I am also mentally checking the position of other aircraft.

You can now see we are well beyond the normal position for base leg, so commencing a level turn use 30° of bank. Rolling out crosswind as in a normal circuit, select half flap, 1500 RPM and trim for 80 Kts. You can already see the aspect of the runway looks rather flat. Checking to the right to clear the approach, we will descend to 500′ in the final turn as we do for a normal landing. Now, rolling out on the centreline of the runway, set 2000 RPM to hold 500′ and 80 Kts. Call:
   Alpha Zulu finals. Flarepath demo."
   "Alpha Zulu, cleared flarepath demo. Call over-shooting."
   "Alpha Zulu.

You can see the runway lights almost appear as two continuous lines, and very flat. We are low, and this is

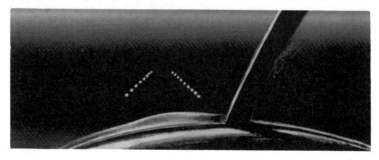

confirmed by the VASIS, which are all red. Watch the lights and the VASIS as we progress in level flight. The near VASIS are now going white; this is the correct glidepath. I will

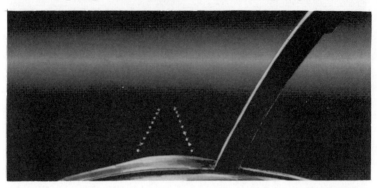

momentarily descend to hold it, so that you can remember the picture. You can just see each individual light and the runway is taking shape. Reapplying power to maintain level flight, as we get closer you can see the VASIS are going white/white and the runway lights stand out clearly. We are high, well above the glidepath.

Overshooting, apply full power, raise the nose into the climbing attitude for 75 Kts. and turn right 20° to get on the dead side. We call:

Alpha Zulu overshooting."
"Alpha Zulu, call downwind."
"Alpha Zulu.

Turning left to parallel the runway, I want you to raise the flap and continue the climb straight ahead to 1000'. Mainly fly visually, but every now and then confirm your attitude on the artificial horizon. At 1000' level off, turn crosswind and fly a normal circuit. I will take over just before turning base leg. Carry out the checks and tell me where you think the other aircraft are positioned. You have control."

STUDENT PRACTISES.

"I have control. Follow me through. Look behind the trailing edge and you can see the threshold at 45°. Checking it is clear to the right and round to the left, make a level turn in the normal manner onto base leg. Rolling out, throttle back to 1500 RPM, check the speed is less than 100 Kts., lower half flap and trim for 80 Kts. Aim to turn finals at 600'. You can use the altimeter to help you, but also try to judge your progress from the aspect of the runway lights. Assess the position of other aircraft. One has just called 'Downwind' and the other is rolling. Looking right to clear the approach, check the altimeter; 600' and we are just approaching the centreline. Using no more than 30° of bank and holding 80 Kts., turn onto finals. Rolling out now, call:

Alpha Zulu finals. No landing light."
"Alpha Zulu, cleared to land. 260°/12 Kts."
"Alpha Zulu.

Immediately lower full flap and trim for 75 Kts. We are a little too high, white/pink on the VASIS and each runway light is clear, so throttle back slightly to regain the glidepath. It now looks better, so hold this picture by adding a little power. We can just see each light, the runway aspect looks good and we have white/red on the VASIS. A quick check on the height, 200', and from here we ignore the VASIS and use the runway shape and lights. Almost over the threshold, look along the runway and try to remember the aspect of the lights for landing. Flaring now —

— throttle closed to hold off by reference to the lights — touching down and keep straight by looking at the lights at the far end.

To roll, smoothly apply full power and keep straight with rudder. Check speed increasing and full power, 2300 RPM. At 60 Kts. make a positive 'unstick'. Rotate now into the climb attitude. Before losing sight of the lights, once again, transfer to instruments and hold the climbing attitude on the artificial horizon. With full flap it is 2° high. Only make small pitch changes to correct the speed. Check the ball is central, altimeter increasing and speed 70 Kts. At 100′ raise the flap to half, maintain the climb attitude for 75 Kts. and check the heading is 270°. At 200′, increase to 80 Kts. and raise the remaining flap. Now continue the climb to 500′. I want you to practise a few circuits without the landing light. Remember to call 'Finals, no landing light'. You have control."

STUDENT PRACTISES.

END OF EXERCISE.

Aircraft Position in Flight Profile

Aircraft on base leg. The instructor has control.

Air Exercise

"This time we will put on the landing light during finals, to see how it affects the landing. It can be useful on a poorly lit airfield, and also ATC like you to use it as they can see you more easily.

Checking right — it is all clear, so we can turn onto finals. Rolling out now, select the light on and call:

Alpha Zulu, finals."

"Alpha Zulu, clear to land. 260°/10 Kts."

"Alpha Zulu.

Now, lowering full flap, trim for 75 Kts., Out here you can see the light has little effect. Wait until we are about 100′. In the meantime we use the VASIS and the runway lights to judge the approach.

Now you can begin to see the threshold, but do not be mesmerised by it. Still use the runway lights to judge your landing flare. Easing into the flare and we are down.

You can see the light does help a little, but don't rely on it for landing. It should only support the basic night technique. We will turn off at those two double lights on the right-hand side, but be careful, there may be other aircraft there. Now, when well clear, stop and call:

Alpha Zulu, clear."

"Alpha Zulu."

"Carry out the after-landing checks and return to dispersal."

STUDENT PRACTISES.

END OF EXERCISE.

EXERCISE 21 — AEROBATICS — RECOVERY FROM THE VERTICAL AND SPIRAL DIVE

NOTES: (1) Selecting half throttle during the recovery from the vertical, is considered to be a reasonable compromise between high gyroscopic forces and the beneficial effect of slipstream.

   (2) This exercise should be practised before the student carries out solo aerobatics.

Aircraft Position in Flight Profile

Aircraft is climbing, with the student flying.

Air Exercise

"Continue the climb to 6000′ and carry out the HASELL checks. Position the aircraft over that disused airfield at 9 o'clock.

Good, I have control. We will start by practising incipient spin recovery. I will carry out a manoeuvre, and directly I say 'You have control', take over and recover into level flight. Is that clear?"

STUDENT ANSWERS

"Follow me through. We will carry out a 180° turn to the left to clear the area. Rolling out now, — 65 Kts., applying full pro-spin control — you have control."

STUDENT PRACTISES.

"Good, stay near the airfield and carry out a further clearing turn. Then I will demonstrate a recovery from the vertical. I have control. Follow me through.

I will dive to 130 Kts. at full throttle. Watch the RPM; 115 Kts. — 2600 RPM, 125 Kts. — 2700 RPM, the red line limit; ease the throttle, remember this speed — 130 Kts., looking up and pulling up — full throttle — see how the speed decreases —

almost in the vertical, and say we have a brain failure; things have gone wrong; the controls do not respond. Recovery — firmly centralise the controls — lock the rudder — half throttle — hold the stick with both hands — there we go forward and to the left — nose through horizon — speed increasing — throttle to idle — level the wings and pull to the nearer horizon.

Not very pleasant; actually, it's not likely to happen with elementary aerobatics. Incidentally, it does no harm to the aircraft providing you keep the controls locked solid.

Now I want you to try that. We will enter the dive in a slightly different fashion. First, select the datum RPM, 2600 for 130 Kts., which will ensure you do not exceed the max. revs. at 130 Kts. during the dive. Then pull up, apply full power and hold the vertical. I will tell you when to recover. First carry out a clearing turn. You have control."

STUDENT PRACTISES.

"Recover now."

STUDENT PRACTISES.

"I have control. That was not too bad was it? Have you any questions?"

STUDENT ANSWERS

"I will now show you the recovery from the steep spiral dive. Follow me through. First a 180° turn to clear the area; all seems clear. Applying full power, and pulling up — now roll and pull through — spiralling down, speed increasing —

recovery — close the throttle — roll to the nearer horizon — now pull to level flight.

Directly your nose inadvertently and significantly drops below the horizon and your speed increases, you must immediately close the throttle. Also, try to look for the nearer horizon, roll towards it, and then pull out of the dive. Any questions?"

STUDENT ANSWERS

"I will now place the aircraft in a spiral dive and I want you to recover when I say 'You have control'. Follow me through. You have control."

STUDENT PRACTISES.

END OF EXERCISE.

EXERCISE 21 — AEROBATICS — THE LOOP

NOTES: (1) In the early stages, it can be easier to select the datum RPM to avoid having to throttle back in the dive to prevent over-speeding the engine.

(2) The average light aircraft loop takes about twelve seconds.

Aircraft Position in Flight Profile

Straight and level at 4000′ AGL.

Air Exercise

"Before practising our first manoeuvre, the loop, I want you to carry out the HASELL checks."

STUDENT PRACTISES.

"Good, it is very important to double-check that you are well strapped-in. Can you see a railway line at 2 o'clock?"

STUDENT ANSWERS

"It is 'out of sun' and will make a good 'line' feature, so that we can check the accuracy of our loop. Follow me through on the controls.

For a final lookout, it is wise to dip the wings to clear the area below. Lining up with the railway, apply full throttle, and dive like this with the nose about 30° below the horizon; trim out the heavier loads — check wings level — ball in the centre, slight left rudder as speed increases — 125 Kts., ease the throttle and check the RPM — we will pull up at 135 Kts. — now brace your stomach, look up and pull fairly hard like this — wings level — full power — maintain the 'G' — right rudder to balance — look horizon

— wings level — pull by 'feel' —   nose low, so half throttle

— speed increasing, pull more 'G' and smoothly ease to level flight. Now throttle back to cruise RPM and trim.

Ideally we look for a constant pitch rate, but in fact the amount you pull is limited at high speed by 'G', and at low speed at the top of the loop, by the stall; in other words we use 'feel'. The transition is progressive from 'G' to 'feel', back to 'G' again, although the stick is gradually moving back until the nose is through the horizon.

We will do another one, and I will now show you pitch control more precisely. First the HELL checks: height above 3000′ — engine T.'s and P.'s, mixture and fuel satisfactory — location, there is our 'anchor' point at 3 o'clock — finally, two 90° turns to clear the area — we will dive along the railway line at 10 o'clock. Follow me through.

This time I will set datum power — 2600 RPM — so we do not have to ease the throttle — diving as before, we are looking for 135 Kts. — now brace the stomach and look up and pull up — full power — note the pitch rate — maintain the 'G' — horizon in view — pulling too tight and there is the 'buffet' — relax the pull, but keep one 'G' — pull by 'feel' — speed increasing, now more 'G', not too much . . . about like this, and smoothly ease into level flight.

Now you try one; I will talk you through it. You have control."

STUDENT PRACTISES.

"I have control. Good, not bad for the first attempt. How do you feel?"

STUDENT ANSWERS

"I now want to show you two mistakes that can be made when looping and how to recover. First the 'buffet', when you do not relax the back pressure. Follow me through.

There is our 'anchor' point, and the area seems clear, so dive as before — looking for 135 Kts. — tighten your stomach, look up and pull up — wings level — full power — pulling harder — there is the horn — almost inverted — pull through the 'buffet' — aircraft shudders and rolls to the left — recovery — centralise controls — wait for speed to increase — now roll wings level with aileron.

In fact, that was the start of the incipient stage of the spin. We did not throttle back as the nose was not too low. How are you feeling?"

STUDENT ANSWERS

"Finally, let us have a look at the other extreme, when we fail to pull hard enough initially, or enter at too low a speed. Follow me through.

Once again clear the area — diving now — this time we will pull up at 110 Kts. — full power — there goes the horn and the 'buffet' — we are vertical — controls ineffective, the nose is dropping, also the wing. Recovery — half throttle — both hands on stick — lock rudder — nose through horizon — speed increasing, so close throttle — look for horizon — roll level and pull to level flight. All I did then was a practical application of a recovery from the vertical.

I hope that this has demonstrated why you must start the loop at the correct speed and power, and learn how to 'feel' your way around, but still maintaining an acceptable pitch rate. Now, I want you to practise recovering from the 'buffet' and the vertical. I will talk you through it. You have control."

STUDENT PRACTISES.

END OF EXERCISE.

EXERCISE 21 — AEROBATICS — BARREL ROLL

NOTES: (1) As with the loop, a datum power setting can be used for the dive.

(2) The average light aircraft barrel roll takes about eleven seconds.

Aircraft Position in Flight Profile

Straight and level flight at 4000'. HASELL checks complete.

Air Exercise

"I have control. Ideally, the barrel roll is a smooth comfortable manoeuvre with a constant rate of roll and pitch. The aircraft should always be in balance, and this requires continuous adjustment of the rudder.

We will roll left, around the cloud at 1 o'clock. Do you see it?"

STUDENT ANSWERS

"Follow me through on the controls. A final lookout to clear the area, set our datum power of 2600 RPM, and dive at 30° like this towards the cloud. Now at 110 Kts. turn 45° to the right, using 40° of bank. Looking for 130 Kts. — pull up and roll left now — full power, left rudder to balance — aim to pull and roll above cloud with wings vertical —

now more aileron for wings level on horizon —

maintain the roll and pull —

now reduce power to level off at start-point.

The classic barrel roll is difficult to follow, so this time we will carry one out from a straight pull-up. During the dive choose a point opposite the wing tip at which to aim, when the wings should be level inverted and the nose is on the horizon. Follow me through.

Two 90° turns to clear the area — now once again set 2600 RPM and dive at 30° — we will roll left — choose a point on the left wing tip — that lake will do — looking for 130 Kts. — ball in the centre — we will pull up straight to 30° above the horizon — pulling up now — full throttle — nose high like this — now roll left — maintain the pull — left rudder to balance — wings vertical — now aim at the lake — increase aileron, less pull — wings level on horizon — keep rolling — combine with pull to level flight — now throttle back.

Notice that the roll was not constant, because I was adjusting it to match the bank with nose position. Once you have recognised the rhythm, you will also be able to achieve a constant rate of roll. Now you try one. I will talk you through it. You have control. Remember your HELL checks."

STUDENT PRACTISES.

END OF EXERCISE.

EXERCISE 21 — AEROBATICS — STALL TURN

Aircraft Position in Flight Profile

Straight and level at 4000'. HASELL checks complete.

Air Exercise

"I have control. We will carry out a stall turn to the left, to take advantage of the effect of slipstream. Let us use that railway line at 10 o'clock, to check our accuracy. Follow me through. Setting the datum power, 2600 RPM, turn right to clear the area — now back along the railway line and dive like this. We are looking for 130 Kts. Trim, and balance with rudder — look up and pulling up as for loop — not quite so hard — wings level — full power — right rudder to balance — look left wingtip for vertical — stick forward to hold the vertical,

maintain it with forward pressure — more right rudder to balance — aircraft stopped, full left rudder — right aileron to stop roll — throttle closed on horizon — dab right rudder to check swing — hold vertical — now pull to level flight.

Quite a pleasant manoeuvre, isn't it?"

STUDENT ANSWERS

"You now have another ace up your sleeve; if you find yourself inadvertently in the vertical, you can sometimes stall turn out.

Before carrying out a stall turn yourself, I want you to practise smoothly applying left rudder in level flight at a low speed, say 70 Kts., at the same time keeping the wings level with the ailerons. This will give you some idea of the co-ordination required. You have control."

STUDENT PRACTISES.

"Good, I have control. There are two other very important points. One, you must hold the aircraft vertical with the elevators. This will entail forward pressure. Two, you must, as the speed decays in the vertical, progressively apply right rudder to balance the aircraft. If you don't, the aircraft will skid sideways in the vertical, and the rudder will be 'blanketed' just when you most need it. Any questions?"

STUDENT ANSWERS

"We will now carry out a stall turn together. You fly the aircraft and I will talk you through it. The actual moment that you apply left rudder is a matter of experience; you don't have time to look at the airspeed. As a guide, after you think it is too late, count 'one-thousand-and-one, one-thousand-and-two, and then apply rudder. Initially, I will tell you. You can make it easier for yourself by always pulling up at the same speed, thereby getting the rhythm of the manoeuvre. Now, carry out a clearing turn and then dive along that road at 10 o'clock. You have control."

STUDENT PRACTISES.

END OF EXERCISE.

EXERCISE 21 — AEROBATICS — SLOW ROLL

Aircraft Position in Flight Profile

Straight and level at 4000'. HASELL checks complete.

Air Exercise

"I have control. In a slow roll the aircraft revolves around the longitudinal axis in level flight. You aim to keep the nose just above a reference point on the horizon, by the combined use of elevators and rudder. Let us use that cloud at 12 o'clock. A final check that your straps are as tight as possible, especially the lap strap; it should almost hurt. We will clear the area by turning 90° right and then return towards the cloud. Follow me through. All seems clear. Do you see the cloud?"

STUDENT ANSWERS

"Opening to full throttle with right rudder to balance, trim for level flight. We will roll to the left. Looking for 125 Kts. Now raise the nose just above the cloud like this, check the

pitch, and with half aileron start rolling now. Right rudder,

238

increasing — more aileron —

stick forward to hold nose above cloud —

now include left rudder —

more left rudder to hold nose up and play stick for direction,

now less aileron and stick coming back —

check roll and smoothly centralise controls.

It is important to prevent the nose dropping below the cloud, especially when becoming inverted.

We will now practise three exercises leading up to the complete roll. We will use the same cloud as our reference point, and I'll roll the aircraft left and right with ever-increasing bank to about 80°, and at the same time keep the nose on the cloud with opposite rudder. I will show you first. Follow me through. Rolling left now — left aileron — right rudder — rolling right — right aileron — left rudder.

Did you notice how I used the rudder to keep the nose on the cloud?"

STUDENT ANSWERS

"Now I want you to practise that. You have control."

STUDENT PRACTISES.

"I have control. Good, now we will do the same thing but inverted. Follow me through. Rolling inverted now, and hold. Notice the nose position. I want you to hold the nose position with wings level and remember the stick force required. You have control."

STUDENT PRACTISES.

"I have control. Now I will roll left and right, using rudder to maintain direction in combination with the stick. Follow me through. Rolling left — left rudder — rolling right — right rudder. Now practise that. You have control."

STUDENT PRACTISES.

"I have control. Rolling out now — we will have a short rest. How do you feel?"

STUDENT ANSWERS

"Yes, aerobatics do require determination.
Let us update the HELL checks. Height 4000′ — T.'s and P.'s and fuel satisfactory — there is our anchor point at 3 o'clock, and finally a 180° turn — all is clear. I will now show you the last 90° of the roll, before practising a complete one.

This is the difficult part, because you are flying with crossed controls. To begin with, most people pull too early and don't apply sufficient opposite aileron to counter the roll effect of rudder. I will first put the aircraft in 'knife-edge' flight to the right, and then roll out to the left as you would complete a normal slow roll. Follow me through. This is 'knife-edge' flight, with lots of top rudder and opposite aileron. Rolling out now — less aileron — stick coming back — wings level — smoothly centralise controls. Not very comfortable was it?"

STUDENT ANSWERS

"That is why we strap in tightly. Now put the aircraft in knife-edge and then roll level. Use that cloud at 11 o'clock as a reference point. You have control."

STUDENT PRACTISES.

"Good, now show me a complete slow roll remembering to clear the area first. I will talk you through it. You have control."

STUDENT PRACTISES.

"I have control. That wasn't too bad. The slow roll is initially difficult and requires lots of practise, especially if you want to do it at low level. I will show you why. Follow me through.

Rolling inverted, check the altimeter — 4000'. Now rolling a bit more, allow the nose to drop slightly like this — continue the roll but pulling too early, we 'dish out' into level flight; look at the altimeter — we have lost 400'.

If you allow the nose to get too low, it can be 'curtains' at low level.

A contributory factor to the height loss, is pulling too early; this is known as 'dishing out'. It is often a sign of panic or disorientation at low level. Do not be too sure that it cannot happen to you. If you do inadvertently allow the nose to get too low, continue to roll but do not pull. I will show you. Follow me through.

Note the height. Rolling inverted, allow the nose to get too low. To recover, continue to roll but do not pull until now. Look at the altimeter, we have still lost 200'. If the nose gets very low, below 30°, also close the throttle.

Now I want you to roll inverted, allow the nose to get too low and then recover. You have control."

STUDENT PRACTISES.

END OF EXERCISE.

EXERCISE 21 — AEROBATICS — ROLL-OFF-THE-TOP

Aircraft Position in Flight Profile

Straight and level at 4500'. HASELL checks complete.

Air Exercise

"I have control. I will now show you how to combine the first half of a loop with a half slow roll when we are inverted; in other words, a 'roll-off-the-top', as I briefed on the ground.

As with a loop, choose a line feature on the ground, with a wing tip into sun if possible; the coastline will do. Turning 90° left and 90° right for a last lookout, set our new datum power of 2500 RPM. It is lower than before, because our entry speed will be higher. There is the coast, so dive at 30°, like this. Looking for 145 Kts., we pull up harder than with a loop — check the ball — brace your stomach — look up and pulling up now — wings level — maintain the 'G' — full power — right rudder — look horizon, anticipate nose just above — now stick forward to hold inverted — now roll out as for slow roll.

Look at the coast, we are facing in the opposite direction and have gained 300'. Now carry out your HELL checks, and then try a roll-off-the-top. I will talk you through it. You have control."

STUDENT PRACTISES.

END OF EXERCISE.

EXERCISE 21 — AEROBATICS — ONE VERTICAL ROLL AND STALL TURN

Aircraft Position in Flight Profile

Straight and level at 5000'. HASELL checks complete.

Air Exercise

"I have control. I will now show you a vertical roll and stall turn. We must dive to 175 Kts., almost the Vne, so we have to be careful not to exceed it, or the maximum RPM. We will therefore ease the throttle progressively after passing 125 Kts. Follow me through.

A final lookout through 180° — now dive like this, fairly steeply. 125 Kts., ease the throttle — ball in the centre — check RPM — trim out the main loads — brace the stomach — 170 Kts. — look up and pull up fairly hard, like this. Wings level — ball central — look at left wing tip for vertical — full power — now vertical, so stick progressively forward — full left aileron — play stick to hold vertical — stop roll with aileron — more right rudder — now full left rudder — right aileron — throttle closed — check swing — hold, and pull out of dive.

The vertical roll requires attention to detail. The wings must be level when you pull through the horizon, with the ball exactly in the centre. You might have to play the stick slightly, backwards and forwards to maintain the wing tip vertical. Ideally, the stick forward movement should be fairly constant. If the wing tip curves up and down through the horizon, the roll is not vertical. You can stop the roll by timing, but it is more accurate to use ground and horizon cues. Now try a vertical roll yourself. The secret is to assess how much forward control column movement is required to keep the aircraft going vertical. To begin with check the aircraft vertically and hold momentarily before rolling. You have control."

STUDENT PRACTISES.

END OF EXERCISE.

EXERCISE 22 — FORMATION FLYING

Aircraft Position in Flight Profile

Aircraft in echelon right at cruising speed in level flight.

Air Exercise

"Watch the lead aircraft and you can see that relative to him we are not moving. This is the Number 2 position in formation.

We judge our position by looking through the wingtip nav. light to the propeller spinner and along the elevator hinge line. Try to imagine those lines, you want to be at the apex of the triangle they form. This gives us the correct fore-and-aft position and half a wingspan separation. Also you want to fly level with the leader; to do this you should just be able to see the air filter under the bottom of the wing. To keep in position we pick up any relative movement and make the necessary corrections. In principle, the cardinal rule, in formation is to never take your eyes off the lead aircraft, and also you must trust him implicitly.

First let us cover fore-and-aft movement; ideally we want to look along the elevator hinge line. We hold position by making small power adjustments; in fact, we also need small elevator and rudder inputs as we change power and speed, but it's easier to ignore them as you're in a fluid situation and will quickly learn to co-ordinate them unconsciously.

Follow me through. Reducing power, look, the leader appears to pull ahead of us. Increase the power a fraction and we have stopped dropping back; add more power and we start to move forward. Here we are approaching the correct position, looking along the hinge line. Anticipating slightly, take off a little power and continue to make small corrections to hold position.

Increasing power and we start to move forward. Be careful as we must not lose sight of our leader. Reducing power and we stop going forward and are now slipping back. Anticipating the correct position, power up to this throttle setting. Feel how I'm holding the position with small throttle movements. At any speed or configuration try to remember the datum throttle position by feel, once you're steady on the leader.

I will fly the aircraft and you can practise holding position fore-and-aft with power. Is that clear?"

STUDENT ANSWERS

"You have control of the throttle."

STUDENT PRACTISES.

"I have control. Good, remember the position we look for, through the nav. light to the spinner and along the elevator hinge line; in the vertical plane we should just see the engine air filter under the bottom of the wing. As with all flying, quick and accurate trimming is the key to success; formation flying is no exception, we must start off in trim.

Follow me through. You can see we're now level, but by easing the stick forward, we go down. We're low and can no longer see our reference points; to regain position ease back on the stick like this. Again a little anticipation is required to stop in the correct position. Similarly, going up we must be careful not to lose sight of our leader; to regain position go down gently.

To maintain the correct references and half span separation we use aileron and rudder. Consequently be careful not to end up with crossed controls. Moving out with aileron, you can see how we seem to move forward even though we are still aligned with the elevator hinge line. To regain position use a little aileron. It is more a matter of thinking the aircraft back into position rather than using too much aileron. Try to make all your corrections smoothly and with small control movements.

Here we are back in position. It is obvious but I'll remind you that you must ignore the dihedral. Also when you are settled take a quick glance at the slip-ball to ensure it is central.

I want you to practise holding position. Remember we talk about moving forwards and backwards, up and down and in and out. To start with, I'll handle the power and when you have settled down I'll give you the throttle as well. Any questions?"

STUDENT ANSWERS

"You have control."

STUDENT PRACTISES.

"I have control. In formation safety is paramount; I have emphasised that you must not lose sight of the leader. It can easily happen if you allow yourself to drift too high. I will demonstrate a 'break' and rejoin. Follow me through. We tell the leader our intention:

"Red 2 for break and rejoin."
"Red 2 clear."

"Now letting the aircraft drift up, we lose sight of the lead aircraft; we must break away. Pull up and rolling to the right, full power and count 1001 — 1002.

Red 2 breaking."
"Red leader, Roger, heading 090 — 100 knots."

Roll the wings level and look for the leader; there he is at 10 o'clock. We leave full power on and drop down to put him on the horizon. We hold him at 11 o'clock in the windscreen and on the horizon. Initially as we close he seems to be almost stationary. Hold this picture and wait.

See, he is growing in size; he is starting to 'blossom' as the fighter pilots say. Throttle back as we have 20 knots overtake and must allow for the aircraft's inertia. Here we are stabilising about 2 wingspans out and a little behind. From here on it is just a matter of creeping back into positon, first fore-and-aft, then up and down and finally in. Put the aircraft back in the correct position and then when you're ready call for a break and rejoin. Is that clear?"

STUDENT ANSWERS

"You have control."

STUDENT PRACTISES.

"I have control. In formation it is essential to try to relax physically, otherwise you will tire quickly. To relax, open up the formation slightly, like this. Use the time to check the fuel, engine instruments and vacuum pressure. Then you can move back into position.

Now let us practise changing position in formation. Remember a further golden rule; never change your formation position except on clear instructions or permission from the leader. In addition, always be aware of the movement of other aircraft in the formation. We tell the leader:

Red 2, clear line astern."

"Red 2 clear."

"We move in at right angles, so throttling back to move astern, drop down slightly. Power on to stabilise, notice we have established an aircraft length between us and the leader and that we are slightly below him. Now move astern with aileron into this position. A little extra power will be

temporarily needed to maintain our fore-and-aft position. To maintain one fuselage length separation we want the tailplane to fill your half of the windscreen. Laterally, you want to be able to see either side of the fuselage, but rather more of your side than mine. Match your bank with the leader's; use him like an artificial horizon. For vertical separation we use the wing walkway; we want to see about 6″ of it just in front of the flap.

I'll demonstrate holding this position, follow me through. First up-and-down; easing forward and immediately the leader goes up and becomes difficult to see. We correct by easing back until we can just see the walkway; remember this. Going a little higher, you can feel the buffet on the fin from the leader's slipstream. To correct, ease forward out of the slipstream and descend until we can just see the first 6″ of the walkway.

Fore-and-aft we use the tailplane for reference, it should fill your half of the windscreen. Reducing power and we slip back. You can see immediately we're too far back — because the tailplane does not fill your half of the windscreen. Watch the tendency to fly too loose; it's sloppy and is difficult to pick up errors. As with echelon we use power to hold our position fore-and-aft, so power on to regain the reference.

Lateral station keeping is the most difficult. We want to be able to see either side of the fuselage, as now. Moving out to the left — we're looking at the wingtip; obviously we're out of position. To correct, use a little aileron and move across smoothly. Anticipate the position — about now, and stop the aircraft.

However, you may find that you over-control on the ailerons like this. Moving out to the right and correcting with left aileron, but overdoing it. There we are slipping out to the other side, correcting again and again we slip through. So stop out here to the right and move more steadily and under control. Smoothly back into the correct position. Anticipation and the matching of the leader's angle of bank are the keys to lateral station keeping in line astern.

If you find yourself slicing from side-to-side, stop on one side and relax. When you are ready, start again; move more slowly and avoid over-controlling. Practise holding this position when I give you control. You have control."

STUDENT PRACTISES.

"I have control. Well done, relax. We'll now go back into echelon, but first we must ask the leader before we move:

Red 2, clear echelon right?"

"Red 2, clear."

"As before, move in right angles, out to the right, but still staying low until we are clear by a fuselage length and half a span. Now, moving up and forward into position, I think we'll ask the leader for some turns:

Red 2, ready for turns."

"Red leader, Roger."

"Follow me through, we wait for the leader's signal. See how he is raising his arm and sweeping it laterally across the cockpit from right to left, which means that the turn will be to the left. Completing the second and third signal, there is a pause and he starts to roll. Power on, easing up and rolling to match his bank. On the outside of the turn we climb a fraction on entry and also we are a little faster.

Steady in the turn, we fly the same reference points and as

we're on the outside of the turn guard against the tendency to slip out and fly wide. Watch the leader for the roll-out signal, a fore-and-aft chopping motion with his arm. There it is; one, two, three, pause and roll out. Immediately reduce the power, match his bank and relax the back pressure to descend, so that on roll- out we're level with the leader. Back in level flight, a quick glance to check that the ball is central and the T.'s and P.'s are in the green.

The next turn should be to the right, which means that we will be on the inside and therefore a little slower than the leader. There's the signal, the arm moving from left to right, the pause and he's rolling. Power off a fraction, match his bank and descend slightly. To stabilise in the turn, apply a bit more power again. Now use the same key points to hold the turn.

This time there is a tendency to slip into the centre of the turn. Remind yourself to fly the references and forget about turning. If the turn takes you through the sun and it blinds you, drop down or back to use the leader to blank it out. Never lose sight of him. There is the roll-out signal, so add a touch of power and roll with the leader, at the same time easing up to stay level with him. You can now try the next few turns yourself. You have control."

STUDENT PRACTISES.

"I have control. I will now show you how to fly the Number 3 position; as I said in the briefing, it is a little more difficult looking across the cockpit. Follow me through:

      Red 2 clear echelon left — left."

"Red 2 clear."

"As with all position changes obtain permission from the leader, then move smoothly like this. Reducing power to drop back and down, check it there with power. Now crossing to the left through the line astern position to stabilise out here, still half a wingspan out and one fuselage length back. Finally, power on and move up into position.

Again we use the same reference points; the nav. light to the propeller spinner and looking along the elevator hinge line. However, from your side it is difficult to see the tailplane, and to compensate, you will find yourself flying a little slack. With practice, though, you will be able to hold the correct position more by the general picture rather than the specific references. You have control."

STUDENT PRACTISES.

END OF EXERCISE.

EXERCISE 22 — FORMATION FLYING — TAKE-OFF

Aircraft Position in Flight Profile

Aircraft moving onto the runway to take up the echelon right position.

Air Exercise

"Follow me through. We taxy on to the runway and slot into the echelon right position; hold the aircraft on the toe-brakes. There's the leader's wind-up signal, so power up to 2000 RPM., check the brakes are holding and the pressures. Give a 'thumb's up' signal on the glareshield so that the leader can see you're ready.

Now watch him, he has raised his arm; wait for the 'chop' — pause and brakes off. Increase the power to hold position and keep straight with rudder. Note his elevator is going up. Now raise the nosewheel together with his; hold it and we'll unstick as a pair.

Maintain position as we accelerate. The leader is making the flap signal; again pause and raise the flap, finally retrim. You can continue the climb. You have control."

STUDENT PRACTISES.

END OF EXERCISE.

EXERCISE 22 — FORMATION FLYING — LANDING

Aircraft Position in Flight Profile

Aircraft in echelon right, with the formation joining on a wide downwind position for a left hand pattern.

Air Exercise

"Here we are joining in a wide downwind position. Remember from the briefing, we fly a wider than normal circuit and just stay in formation on the leader. He will make the radio calls but will not call or signal turns or power changes.

See the leader's hand up, flap, flap, go — pause — drop a hand onto the flap lever and set take-off flap. Check the position and retrim. Now quickly run through the normal pre-landing checks. Brakes off, mixture rich, carb. air hot, fuel pump on, contents sufficient, flap set, harness locked, canopy closed and carb. air cold. When the leader looks at you give a thumbs up signal to show that your checks are complete.

He's looking now, so thumbs up. Shortly we should be turning onto base leg, this turn will not be signalled. The leader is starting to roll, following him. It is only a short turn, as we roll out anticipate the power reduction. Even so we're just starting to move forward, so back with the power. Obviously the leader has throttled back and we should retrim as the speed is lower. Standing by for the finals turn.

Banking with the leader, again adding a little power to hold position. Now rolling out, power back slightly. We can expect a radio call for flap."

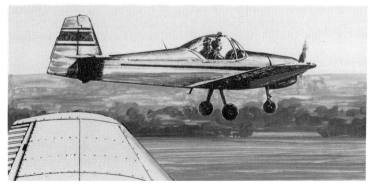

255

"Red, full flap, full flap, go."

"Select full flap down and retrim. From now on be prepared to use the throttle positively to hold position. Also start glancing from the leader to the runway. Remember we aim to complete an individual landing on the right half of the runway. You can see the threshold coming up and the leader is starting to flare. Stay with him and wait for the call."

"Red, cut, cut."

"Now throttle back and land normally. Brake to establish nose-to-tail separation and slow down a little more than the leader, as he will want to cross over to the right to clear the runway. We'll call when there is sufficient separation and we are sure we can stop safely:

Red leader clear cross."

"Red leader."

"Even though we have landed we're still part of the formation, and as we will be the last aircraft to clear the runway we make the call for the formation:

Red formation clear.

Finally we taxy back in as a unit until we are on the apron and stationary."

END OF EXERCISE.

EXERCISE 22 — FORMATION FLYING — BREAK AND STREAM LANDING.

NOTES   (1) Stream landings with all the aircraft tracking down on the centreline are becoming more normal with nosewheel aircraft, rather than the practise of landing alternatively left/right.

        (2) When in echelon as a No. 3, it is much better to also use the leader as a reference to cut down any whip effect. This technique was highlighted by the famous Black Arrows, the Hunter aerobatic team of No. 111 (F) Squadron. They used the term "sophisticated formation flying."

Aircraft Position in Flight Profile

Aircraft in the Number 3 position in Vic formation on the extended centreline of the active runway.

Air Exercise

"We're on the Tower frequency, and if you look well ahead you can see the airfield about 4 miles away. As we are in echelon left we must cross to the other side, but wait until we are told"

      "Red formation echelon right, go."

"That's for us; the Number 2 is already in position. Power back to slip aft to establish nose-to-tail separation on the Number 2. Also ease down below the others to avoid their slipstream. Now power on and move across to the right. Passing astern the Number 2, check the movement to the right to stop the correct distance out from him. Finally power on again and move forward and up into position.

Now hold this position, ride any turbulence and look both at the leader as well as the Number 2 to damp down any of his oscillations. You want the formation to look tidy. The end of the runway is coming up, so wait for the call."

      "Red breaking."

"Count 1000 — 2000 — there goes No. 2 — 3000 — 4000 —

now it's us — full power, roll and pull to follow the others. Match our bank angle with theirs. We should be evenly spaced and aim to hold them both on the horizon. Use coarse aileron if necessary. Look at the runway; we are downwind, so power back to 2200 RPM. Don't forget the downwind checks. Brakes off, mixture rich, carb. air hot, fuel pump on, contents sufficient, flap up, harness locked, canopy closed and carb. air cold. Look where the leader turns in; make sure the Number 2 follows him and we'll turn at the same place.

Turning in about now, use a gentle continuous curve onto finals. The leader is landing in the middle and shortly he'll move over on to the downwind side of the runway. Number 2 is landing and our spacing looks good. We call:

Red 3 finals."

"Red 3 land, 2 on."

"Red 3.

We make a normal landing and like the others take the middle of the runway. Starting to flare — touch down and lower the nose. Check brakes working and slow down. Now move onto the downwind side to leave the other half of the runway free in case anyone following has a brake failure or wants to go round again. Is that all clear?''

STUDENT ANSWERS

END OF EXERCISE.

EXERCISE 22 — FORMATION FLYING — TAILCHASING

Aircraft Position in Flight Profile

Aircraft at altitude in echelon right and the leader has called for a tailchase.

Air Exercise

"The leader has called 'Standby for tailchase', so we can expect him shortly to 'break up' and to the left. Follow me through. I'll count for 2 seconds and then follow him. Remember in the briefing, I said that we aim to follow him using a constant power setting."

"Red section, follow me, go."

"Count 1001, 1002 and away we go. The leader is about ⅓ of the way up the windscreen; we hold him there and follow his movements at the same place in the sky as he made them. A

quick glance to confirm we have 2300 RPM set. The leader is diving and pulling away from us; this 'stretching' is normal in a dive. Now he's rolling left and pulling up. We follow him and as we go up we appear to be closing; again this is normal as the speed is decreasing.

Starting a further gentle dive, to close the gap pull the nose up to place the leader at the bottom of the windscreen. You can see how we are catching up. In fact, I am now too close; ideally we aim for 100 yards separation, so I must widen the gap.

260

Releasing the pull, let him drift up the windscreen. I'll hold him there, just over halfway up, and you can see we are stretching the line. Stopping there, once again pull him back $\frac{1}{3}$ of the way up the windscreen.

I'll give you control shortly. Try to hold this position and follow each of his manoeuvres at the same place in the sky. If you hit the slipstream, don't forget you have the rudder to help you roll. With experience you may find it easier to fly slightly out to one side. At the end of the tailchase the leader will level his wings and then rock them to signal that he wants you to join in close again. A final point; even though we are trying to do this with constant power, don't be afraid to use throttle if necessary. You have control."

STUDENT PRACTISES.

END OF EXERCISE.

EXERCISE 23 — MULTI-ENGINE — ASYMMETRIC PART I

NOTE: (1) We feather the engines from right to left, i.e. mixture, propeller, throttle, for the following reasons:—

(a)It is more systematic.

(b)It confirms to the Fire Drill.

(c)It is kinder to the counter balance weights. If, by chance, the wrong mixture is closed, it can always be opened again, as if it is a throttle.

Aircraft Position in Flight Profile

3000′ in the cruise.

Air Exercise

"I have control. Asymmetric Part I, but first I will carry out the HASELL checks. Height — we must be above 3000′ AGL when flying on one engine. Airframe — we should not be too heavy, such that our performance will be critical if we cannot restart the engine. Security — the seat should always be adjusted so that we can easily apply full rudder. Engine — cowl flaps working, we know the systems and are familiar with the restarting procedure in the circumstances; in other words we should consider the temperature, the humidity and other relevant factors. Location — it is sensible to be within a reasonable distance of an airfield and the weather should be acceptable. Lookout — we must avoid being too engrossed with cockpit indications.

I will now feather one engine, and show you that under normal circumstances this aircraft flies quite well and safely on one engine. Sit back and watch how I shut down the left engine — you can now see the left propeller is stationary and feathered to reduce drag.

Nevertheless, to maintain a reasonable speed, we must increase the power on the live engine, and trim. Releasing the controls, you can see the aircraft is stable and maintains 115 Kts. on 75% power. Now you try some turns. You will find that it is easier to roll towards the dead engine than the live one. You have control."

STUDENT PRACTISES.

"We monitor the T.'s and P.'s of the live engine more than usual, as it is working quite hard. We also make certain the fuel is correctly balanced. As you can see, there is no problem in flying the aircraft, as long as we have height and speed in hand.

I will now restart the dead engine. I have control. It is quite easy, provided you use the right technique. Later, I will show you the complete drill for feathering and restarting. To save wear and tear on the engine, allow the cylinder head temperature to start indicating before synchronising the throttles.

Now let us get down to the 'meat' of the exercise. First, we will examine the symptoms of an engine failure in the cruise. Here we are trimmed, hands and feet off the controls. I am now going to throttle back the left engine, simulating a failure. I want you to note what happens. Watch the nose; throttling back now — immediately the nose yaws to the left, followed by a roll to the left, and finally a spiral dive. To recover — open up the dead engine thereby restoring symmetrical power — we can now regain level flight.

Did you notice the sequence?"

STUDENT ANSWERS

"Yes, the aircraft yawed and rolled in the direction of the failed engine. Now let us do the same thing with the other engine, but this time I want you to also look at the turn-and-slip indicator as well as the nose. Closing the right throttle — the nose yaws right, confirmed by the turn indicator — the ball shows a slip towards the live engine — we roll into a spiral dive. Recovering — this time by closing the live engine throttle — control is restored, and we can ease to a steady glide.

Lesson learned; it is better therefore, if we have an engine failure and there is no alternative, to force-land under control rather than continue in a spiral dive. Always keep this in the back of your mind. Opening the power — we are once again back in cruise flight.

This time we will look at the symptoms of an engine failure in turns. Let us start with one to the left. Looking left — all is clear, so entering the turn I will close the outside or right engine — like this — immediately we roll out of the turn, simultaneously skidding to the left; if we continue, it will spiral dive to the right. Instead set equal power, and control is regained.

Now let us carry out a turn to the right, and this time I will close the inside or right engine. Entering the turn — now closing the right throttle — the nose yaws right and the bank quickly increases — we try to stop it with aileron; controls badly crossed; we could run out of aileron and possibly even spin — once again we can regain control by opening up the dead engine to balance the power. Clearly it is worse for the inboard engine to fail in a turn, than the outer one.

As a summary, therefore, of the symptoms of an engine failure, there is a yaw towards the failed engine, and a slip towards the live engine, followed by a roll in the same direction as the yaw, and finally a spiral dive.

Try casting your mind back to your early flying days and tell me if you can remember an exercise that reminds you of these symptoms?"

STUDENT ANSWERS

"Yes, they are similar to the 'further effects of rudder.' I want you to remind yourself of this by trimming the aircraft for straight and level, and then apply rudder without holding the stick. You have control."

STUDENT PRACTISES.

"I have control. You can see it is very similar to the effects of an engine failure, and it is therefore not unreasonable to deduce that the best control to counteract the effect of an engine failure is the rudder. I will now go through the initial action to be taken to regain control when you have an engine failure. Follow me through.

Once again in the cruise, I will simulate a failure of the left engine by throttling back, like this. Recovery — check the yaw with rudder — roll the wings level with the ailerons — confirm the ball is central, and if necessary, increase the power on the live engine to maintain a reasonable speed.

I must emphasise that it is most important to check that the ball is central, as it is our only positive criterion of control.

Now I will close the throttles at random, whilst you check the yaw with rudder and keep the wings level with the ailerons. Always confirm that the ball is central. Don't be too hasty to apply rudder; ascertain the yaw first. You have control."

STUDENT PRACTISES.

"I have control. Quite good, I will now demonstrate the recovery in a turn. Follow me through. First, we will fail the inboard engine. Turning left, I will throttle back the left engine, like this. Recovery — right rudder to check the yaw — now roll the wings level with aileron at the same time checking that the ball is central. Once the wings are level, if necessary increase the power on the live engine. It is most important to check the ball is central, because, if we still have some residual slip, aileron effectiveness can be severely impaired.

This time I will fail the outboard engine. Turning left, I am going to throttle back the right engine, like this — the yaw is not so obvious and helps the roll out of the turn, but we must still apply left rudder to balance the aircraft, and finally check the wings level with aileron. Once again, if necessary add power on the live engine.

Now you turn the aircraft either way, and I will close one of the throttles and you recover to level, balanced flight. You have control."

STUDENT PRACTISES.

"I have control. The next step is to identify the failed engine. At low level this is critical, because it has to be done properly and above all correctly first time. In principle, don't use the instruments as they can be deceptive. Instead, use the catchphrase 'Dead leg — dead engine.'

Setting up the cruise again, I want you to cover up the throttles with this map so I cannot see them, and then close a throttle on me. Do you understand?"

STUDENT ANSWERS

"Now close a throttle. Recovery, right rudder — wings level — ball central. My left leg is not doing any work; you must have closed the left engine. Now take away the map — there, as if by magic, the left throttle is closed.

Setting up the cruise again, I will cover the throttles and then close an engine on you. Take recovery action, identify the failed engine and tell me what you are doing. You have control."

STUDENT PRACTISES.

"I have control. Finally, to complete the initial recovery action, we trim out the rudder loads, but only after the failed engine has been identified. Follow me through. Closing the right engine and applying left rudder, turn the front of the trim wheel in the direction of the load, in this case to the left. In normal flight it is possible to trim out all the loads, like this.

Now I want you to practise the complete initial recovery action. I will cover the throttles and simulate failing engines on a random basis. You have control."

STUDENT PRACTISES.

"I have control. If we are at a safe altitude, we can now check why the engine has failed, using our check list or the familiar mnemonic 'FICT'. Fuel — pump on, check contents, change tanks if necessary. Ignition — check mags. on. Carb. air — select alternate air and mixture rich. Temperatures and pressures — normal.

If, however, the engine RPM starts to run down quickly, it may get too low for feathering, so we have to bear this in mind. Similarly, if there is a fire or an obvious mechanical fault, we should shut the engine down immediately. I will now show you how.

Work from right to left on the engine control console, closing the appropriate lever for the failed engine. Do not try to analyse it; do it 'by numbers'. For example, I will now feather the right engine, like this. Close the right mixture control — the right pitch lever, making certain to bring it through the 'gate', or indent to the feathered position — and finally close the right throttle.

You can now see that the right engine has stopped and is feathered. To secure both engines, use the check list or apply the mnemonic DENFIVES. D for drag — make certain that the flaps are up and that the cowl flaps on the dead engine are closed. EN for engine — temperatures and pressures; make certain that the cowls are correctly set for the live engine; remember that the engine will be working harder than normal especially during the climb, and therefore the T.'s and P.'s should be closely monitored. F for fuel — turn off the fuel and the pump of the dead engine. Make absolutely certain you are not turning off the live engine; it has happened before now. So look outside and say to yourself, 'Right engine has stopped, right fuel off'. Now, if necessary, crossfeed the fuel from the dead side. I for ignition — check mags. on for the live engine and then turn them off on the failed engine. As for the fuel, it is imperative you do it by numbers; it is easy for the mind to get 'scrambled'. Looking outside, right engine failed — right mags. off. V for vacuum — check that we have vacuum on the live engine. E for electrics — turn off the generator on the dead engine and check the load on the live engine. Finally, S for systems — check if we have lost any, in particular the hydraulics which we may require for landing.

I will now show you how to restart the failed engine; we can apply the mnemonic FITMP, or use the checklist. F for fuel — turn on the fuel for the dead engine, the crossfeed off, and fuel pump on. I for ignition — both mags. on for the dead engine. T for throttle — open about a quarter of an inch. M for mixture — open to the fully rich position to prime for two or three seconds, and then close it. P for pitch — open to the cruise position to prevent possible over-speeding. Now pressing the starter, open the mixture gradually when the engine fires; sometimes you have to 'play it'. Momentarily the manifold pressure stays high. Now it has dropped and you can see that the propeller is out of feather. Check the oil pressure, and once it is in the green, open the throttle to about 15″ to allow the engine to warm up gradually until the cylinder head temperature is indicating. We can assist this by throttling back the live engine to a similar setting to slow the aircraft down.

That is the complete engine failure procedure at a safe altitude. Later, we will carry out the engine failure after take-off which requires a slightly modified procedure.

I now want you to shut down the left engine and then restart it. Tell me exactly what you are doing. Don't be too hasty. I will never forgive you if you turn off the mags. on the live engine. You have control."

STUDENT PRACTISES.

"I have control. Good, that wasn't too bad. We will now examine how airspeed and power affect the controlability of the aircraft on one engine.

First let us look at the effect of airspeed. Follow me through. Throttling back the right engine, and setting 75% power or 24" on the live one, I will trim the elevators for a speed of 115 Kts.; it does not matter if we climb or descend slightly — notice I have not trimmed out the rudder loads. I will take charge of the control column and you take control of the rudder, so place your feet on the pedals and hold the aircraft in balance. I am now going to reduce the speed by raising the nose, and I want you to keep the ball in the centre with the use of rudder. Raising the nose now, the speed decreases. Do you have to apply more rudder or less rudder?"

STUDENT ANSWERS

"Yes, more rudder; remember that. Now, lowering the nose, the speed increases. How much rudder do you have to apply this time?"

STUDENT ANSWERS

"Yes, less rudder is required. In other words, for a given power setting, as the speed increases you require less rudder, and if the speed decreases you require more rudder. Remember this.

Now we will have a look at the effect of power. This time I will set 20″ on the live engine, like this. Whilst I maintain 110 Kts. by raising or lowering the nose with the elevators, you open to full power on the live engine, simultaneously keeping the aircraft balanced with rudder. Do you understand?"

STUDENT ANSWERS

"Now open up the live engine."

STUDENT PRACTISES.

"Are you using more or less rudder?"

STUDENT ANSWERS

"Yes, more rudder as the power increases at a constant speed. Still keeping the aircraft balanced, I want you to throttle back the live engine to about 15″, whilst I continue to maintain 110 Kts."

STUDENT PRACTISES.

"How much rudder this time?"

STUDENT ANSWERS

"Yes, much less. In other words more power, more rudder; less power, less rudder.
I have control. What, therefore, do you consider is the worst possible combination of power and speed?"

STUDENT ANSWERS

"Yes, a high power setting and a low speed. In the next exercise, Asymmetric Part II, we will examine this in more detail.

That is the end of Asymmetric Part I. Now fly me back to base and carry out a circuit and landing. You have control."

STUDENT PRACTISES.

END OF EXERCISE.

EXERCISE 23 — MULTI-ENGINE — ASYMMETRIC PART II

NOTE: (1) The purpose of demonstrating thc EFATO at 75% power, is to impress on the student the necessity of opening the live engine to full power.

Aircraft Position in Flight Profile

Straight and level flight at 3000'.

Air Exercise

"I have control. First I want you to carry out the HASELL checks applicable to asymmetric flight."

STUDENT PRACTISES.

"Good, I will now demonstrate Asymmetric Part II. Can you remember from Part I, the worst combination of power and speed?"

STUDENT ANSWERS

"Yes, a high power and a low speed. This leads us on to critical speeds, which are the lowest speeds on one engine that it is possible to maintain control for any given power setting and configuration. First, we will assess the critical speed when the right engine is at full power and the left engine is at idle and windmilling. Follow me through.

We set the aircraft up in level flight like this. Apply maximum power on the right engine, throttle to idle on the left,. check the yaw with rudder, keep the wings level and finally trim. Now, with one hand on the live engine throttle, gradually raise the nose to reduce the speed; keep the ball central by progressively applying right rudder, and at the same time keep the wings level with aileron. The rudder loads are high, so take full advantage of the rudder trim; continue to keep the ball in the centre with the wings exactly level, until you reach full rudder deflection and the ball begins to move. Watch the nose — the aircraft is beginning to yaw uncontrollably — note the speed, 78 Kts. Recovery — stick forward and reduce power simultaneously.

78 Kts. therefore, is the critical speed with the wings level in this configuration for this aircraft at this height.

I hope you noted the recovery action. If we had not acted promptly the aircraft could well have spun. If it does incipient spin, close the throttle immediately; this is why we always have one hand on the live throttle, in particular when flying at low speed on one engine, and also why we have height in hand. If you fly an aircraft which has a critical speed below the stall, recover when the horn sounds a steady note, or at the buffet.

I now want you to find the wings-level critical speed with the left engine still throttled back, but with the right one at 75% power. Do you understand?"

STUDENT ANSWERS

"You have control."

STUDENT PRACTISES.

"I have control. What was the critical speed this time?"

STUDENT ANSWERS

"Yes, it was much less, proving what I said in the briefing that critical speed varies directly with power.

Now, you find the wings-level critical speed with the left engine at full power and the right at zero thrust, with 10″ of manifold pressure set. This simulates the propeller in feather. Take note of the speed when the nose yaws. You have control."

STUDENT PRACTISES.

"Did you notice the speed?"

STUDENT ANSWERS

"Yes, it was lower than our first test at full power because the dead engine was producing less drag.

Now let us look at a particular type of critical speed called the Vmca. The profile is with the worst engine windmilling, in this case the left, the right at full power and the aircraft in the take-off configuration; in other words the undercarriage should be retracted and for this aircraft, take-off flap selected. We are also allowed to use up to 5° of bank towards the live engine. I will now demonstrate this to you.

First get the aircraft well set up. Apply full power on the right engine with the left at idle. Lower take-off flap, trim for level flight and check the ball is in the centre. Follow me through. Now, very gradually reduce the speed by raising the nose, keeping one hand on the throttle of the live engine, and the wings level with the ailerons. Maintain the ball central with the rudder, using the trimmer to the full extent. Anticipate rolling on 5° of bank, 10 Kts. higher than the expected Vmca; this is to avoid adverse yaw at the critical moment. 84 Kts., now apply the 5° of bank — prevent yaw with rudder — check angle of bank on the artificial horizon — hold it with increasing aileron — continue to prevent yaw with rudder as the speed reduces; we are now running out of rudder, speed 74 Kts. and the aircraft yaws out of control. Recovery — stick forward and throttle back simultaneously, and allow the speed to build up.

We lost control at 74 Kts. and this therefore, is the Vmca for this aircraft. Now try that. The secret is to approach it very gradually. You have control."

STUDENT PRACTISES.

"I have control. Under British regulations we never fly to the Vmca, but instead use the safety speed which is always above the Vmca, and for that matter the stall speed. We will now see how it works in practise. Can you remember the safety speed from the briefing?"

STUDENT ANSWERS

"Yes, it is 82 Kts. for this aircraft with take-off flap selected. Now you climb the aircraft at the safety speed with both engines at full power. When you are settled, I will simulate failing an engine, and you maintain control above the safety speed; to do this, you will have to lower the nose slightly. You have control."

STUDENT PRACTISES.

"I have control. How did you find that?"

STUDENT ANSWERS

"Yes, it is relatively easy, provided you maintain the safety speed. Lesson learned; whenever you fly on one engine **never** allow the speed to decay below the safety speed.

We now come to the final and most critical test of all; the engine failure after take-off situation. This combines all the lessons we have learned in the previous asymmetric exercises. I will now demonstrate one to you from the 75% climb in the take-off configuration, or in other words with take-off flap selected and the undercarriage retracted. I want you to close a throttle on me once I am settled in the climb, at the single engine climb speed of 95 Kts. Cover the throttle console with a map, so that I cannot see which throttle you are going to close. I am now ready."

(STUDENT CLOSES ONE OF THE THROTTLES).

"1. Check the yaw with rudder — all engine levers forward — wings level with ailerons — lower the nose like this, to maintain the safety speed — check the ball is central.
2. Dead leg — dead engine; right engine has failed — check for fire — close right mixture, right pitch, right throttle.
3. Increase the speed to the flap up take-off safety speed, 88 Kts.; slightly lower the nose like this — now raise the flaps, still maintaining the new safety speed.
4. Trim the rudder; turn wheel to the left.
5. Secure the aircraft — DENFIVES — you carry them out."

STUDENT PRACTISES.

"You have control. Now restart the dead engine, and set yourself up in the 75% power climb in the take-off configuration at 95 Kts. Tell me when you are ready and I will fail an engine on you and you carry out the full procedure."

STUDENT PRACTISES.

"I have control. Quite good. Periodically we will be practising that, using touch drills.

I will now show you a 'trick of the trade' once you are safely established in the climb, but not until then.

To increase the rate of climb on one engine, you can allow the ball to deviate approximately one ball-width towards the dead engine, like this; counter the yaw with the bank, up to 5° towards the live engine. Although the controls are crossed, the fuselage is producing less drag. It requires fairly fine flying and should only be done at a safe altitude. The rate of climb is increased by approximately 10%. Now you continue with the climb. You have control."

STUDENT PRACTISES.

276

"I have control. Finally, I will demonstrate an engine failure when overshooting with full flap and undercarriage down from a normal approach. Follow me through.

Here we are on a normal approach at 90 Kts. Overshooting now, full throttle — engine fails — check yaw — lower nose — drag flap up — undercarriage up — check ball central — safety speed 82 Kts. — dead foot, dead engine — feather right engine. Now we continue as for a normal engine failure after take-off.

It is most important to raise the drag flap immediately as it can severely impair rudder authority, and with most aircraft will induce a considerable roll towards the dead engine, due to slipstream effect. You should also lower the nose onto the horizon and raise the undercarriage, as speed is the key factor.

Now set the aircraft up on a normal approach with undercarriage and flap down, and when you overshoot I will simulate failing an engine on you. You have control."

STUDENT PRACTISES.

END OF EXERCISE.

EXERCISE 23 — MULTI-ENGINE — ZERO THRUST

NOTE: (1) On some aircraft it may be necessary to adjust the standard zero thrust setting whilst in the circuit, particularly on base leg and finals.

Aircraft Position in Flight Profile

Aircraft at 3500' in the cruise at 120 Kts.

Air Exercise

"I have control. As we discussed on the ground, we do not practise single-engine flying with one engine feathered below 3000' AGL for safety's sake. However, we can simulate the conditions realistically by setting an engine to give zero thrust, although it can vary to a certain extent according to the configuration and speed. Let us find the correct setting for a typical circuit speed, 120 Kts.

The air is quite smooth so we will stay at this altitude. However, to be absolutely realistic, we will use 115 Kts. IAS to take into account the density altitude. First, I want you to feather the starboard engine, please. You have control."

STUDENT PRACTISES.

"Now, find the exact power setting for the right engine to give 115 Kts. in level flight. As a rough guide, 20" and 2400 RPM should do — you are lucky, it seems to be correct. Now restart the starboard engine and then set its power so that we continue to maintain 115 Kts. It may require some fairly fine adjustments, and you must allow the speed to settle down."

STUDENT PRACTISES.

"Good, 10" seems correct and it also ties up with the Manual figure. However, remember this zero thrust is only really accurate for 120 Kts. at 1000'. In fact, you may find me adjusting the thrust very slightly during asymmetric circuits, especially on base leg."

END OF EXERCISE.

278

EXERCISE 23 — MULTI-ENGINE — TAXYING

Aircraft Position in Flight Profile

Aircraft on the apron. Taxy clearance has been given.

Air Exercise

"Taxying is basically the same as for a single-engined aircraft. However, remember we are bigger and weigh more, so watch the wingtips in confined spaces and allow for the increased inertia when stopping. I have control. Follow me through.

To commence taxying, first check it is clear on both sides and ahead, bring the throttles to idle and release the brakes. Now open the throttles together very slightly, and once we are moving, close the throttles and check the brakes both sides. Mine work satisfactorily; try yours."

STUDENT PRACTISES.

"Good, moving forward again, reduce the power slightly to hold this speed. Normally we steer the aircraft with the nosewheel and operate the throttles as a single unit, like this. However, be careful you don't inadvertently apply brake whilst turning; this is very easily done, especially when heavily loaded on tarmac. As a safeguard, put your heels on the floor.

To make turning easier at low speeds, we can use differential power. I will show you. To turn to the left, throttle back the left engine and open up the right, at the same time steering with the rudder. You can see the smaller radius of turn. To stop the turn, open the left engine slightly and throttle back on the right, like this. However, avoid using excessive power on the outer engine as you might strain the nosewheel and scrub the tyre.

To stop the aircraft, close the throttles and gently apply the brakes. Now you continue to taxy out, but remember to think ahead. You have control."

STUDENT PRACTISES.

END OF EXERCISE.

279

EXERCISE 23 — MULTI-ENGINE — NORMAL CIRCUIT AND LANDING

Aircraft Position in Flight Profile

Aircraft at the take-off point, with the checks complete.

Air Exercise

"I have control. Follow me through. Before we ask for take-off clearance, let us run through the take-off emergency drills. If we have an engine failure below the safety speed, close both throttles and land on the runway. If we have attained the safety speed below 200′ but cannot land back on again, raise the undercarriage and continue to climb to 200′ before lifting the flap. Do you understand?"

STUDENT ANSWERS

"Springfield, Alpha Zulu ready for departure."
"Alpha Zulu, you are cleared to take-off. Wind 260°/10 Kts."
"Alpha Zulu.

A final look to clear the approach; it is all clear, so we taxy on to the runway in the normal manner and roll forward on the centreline to straighten the nosewheel, apply the brakes and check the DI that we are on the correct runway.

Now open up to 17″ with both throttles and synchronise the power. Holding the control column central, look well ahead, release the brakes, heels on the floor and, keeping straight with rudder open both throttles together to full power. Check speed increasing and full power. Now bring the control column slightly aft to relieve the nosewheel. We will rotate at 74 Kts. Rotating now — hold this attitude and wait for 82 Kts., the safety speed. 82 Kts., so apply the brakes and retract the undercarriage. Maintain the climb, but allow the speed to increase to the blue line, 95 Kts. Trim to hold it. At 200′ raise the flaps and simultaneously hold the attitude against the change of trim. Allow the speed to increase to the cruise climb, 120 Kts. — now throttle back to 24″ and reduce the RPM to

2400. Synchronise the power and retrim to hold 120 Kts.

Approaching 500', look to the right and around to the left, and turn, using 15° of bank. Lower the nose slightly to hold 120 Kts. Rolling out crosswind, you see we are climbing quite quickly and must anticipate levelling at 1000', earlier than in most single-engined aircraft. 900' coming up, so smoothly level off and throttle back to 16" to hold 120 Kts. Retrim. Almost immediately, we are ready to turn downwind; you can see the tail is over the runway. Looking right and left, enter the turn using 30° of bank. Aim to roll out with the wing tip running down the runway. If necessary, adjust the power for 120 Kts. and the attitude to hold 1000'. We call:

Alpha Zulu, downwind."

"Alpha Zulu, clear to finals, number 2."

"Alpha Zulu.

Downwind checks; brakes off — undercarriage down below 140 Kts.; check green lights — mixture rich — cowls closed — pitch, 2400 RPM — fuel, sufficient and pumps on — flap, lower take-off flap, hold the attitude — harness tight and doors closed.

Retrim and maintain the height as the speed reduces. Aim for not less than 95 Kts. before turning base leg. Adjust the power if necessary, but we are doing alright. Now look right and left, and with the threshold 45° behind the trailing edge, turn onto base leg. Use 30° of bank and maintain level flight. Rolling out now to allow for the wind, reduce the power to 12" manifold pressure and trim for 95 Kts. We aim to turn finals at 600', but anticipate earlier as we are a little faster than most light singles. Looking right to clear the approach, turn now, using not more than 30° of bank, and lower the nose to hold 95 Kts. Anticipate rolling out slightly earlier. Rolling out now, check undercarriage down, set the pitch to fully fine and lock the nose just short of the threshold. Call:

Alpha Zulu, finals."

"Alpha Zulu, cleared to land. Wind 260°/10 Kts."

"Alpha Zulu.

Immediately lower full flap and trim for 90 Kts. We hold this picture all the way in. Speed and glidepath control is conventional, but try to anticipate power adjustments; keep them small and do not allow trim changes with power to override your attitude. Similarly, pitch adjustments are small but positive. Also, try to synchronise the power by monitoring the manifold pressure. Now that our glidepath is established and we are getting closer, bring the boundary into your scan. Aim to cross the threshold at 50' and at the Vref., 83 Kts., so we must reduce power slightly and raise the nose a fraction. A final glance at the speed — 83 Kts. Now concentrate outside for the flare. Do not close the throttles early. Flaring now — smoothly close the throttles to hold off with the stick coming back to touch down on the main wheels. Now, gently lower the nosewheel — keep straight with rudder — check throttles closed and with the stick coming back brake if necessary. When reasonably slow, clear the runway and stop for the after-landing checks. Flaps up, but be careful you do not have a 'brain failure' and raise the undercarriage; it has happened before. Fuel pump off — pitot head off — open the cowls.

Now you taxy back to the take-off point. You have control."

STUDENT PRACTISES

END OF EXERCISE.

EXERCISE 23 — MULTI-ENGINE — ASYMMETRIC CIRCUIT AND LANDING

NOTES (1) It is appreciated that with some aircraft it might be wise to lower the undercarriage at the end of the downwind leg. However, this does conflict with the continuity of the downwind checks and should be borne in mind.

(2) The main significance of lowering full flap can be a deterioration in rudder effectiveness, and a tendency to roll towards the dead engine; in other words, the safety speed is no longer valid. Full flap should therefore be applied with caution on finals.

(3) If applicable, carb. air should be left in hot on the zero thrust engine during circuits.

(4) The merit of not using the rudder trim after the downwind leg, is that foot loads are reduced if significant power increases are required on the final approach. We appreciate that not everybody will agree with this, but it is worth considering.

(5) We think that from a training point of view anyway, it is realistic to add 5 Kts. to the 1.3vs threshold speed.

Aircraft Position in Flight Profile

Aircraft at 2000′ prior to joining the circuit. The instructor has control.

Air Exercise

"I will now show you an asymmetric circuit and landing. We will simulate a failure by setting the left engine to zero thrust, with the propeller fully fine and the throttle adjusted to give 10″ manifold pressure. On the live engine we select a low cruise power, 20″ and 2400 RPM, which will also be suitable for the downwind leg. Finally, trim out the rudder loads to keep the ball central. Don't worry if I adjust the zero thrust slightly during the final approach.

If we had a genuine engine failure, before joining the circuit we would call ATC and declare an emergency:

> Springfield, Golf Alpha Romeo Alpha Zulu joining from the South at 2000′. Simulated engine failure."
>
> "Alpha Zulu you are cleared to join. Runway 270° left, QFE 1012."
>
> "Alpha Zulu, 27 left, QFE 1012.

We can now pick the most suitable runway, taking into account the surface wind and the runway length.

Obviously, whilst approaching the field we maintain height as long as possible, take the opportunity to review the emergency, and consider how it will affect the aircraft systems, the hydraulics, fuel and power. Also complete the field approach checks early, and don't forget to inform any passengers of the situation. Using the LIFE mnemonic, we know our location, the instruments are functioning and set the QFE 1012. Check the fuel to feed the right engine, pump on, and balance if necessary, by cross-feeding. Check the T.'s and P.'s, mixture rich and the cowlings closed, unless the temperatures are high.

We will let down well in advance on the dead side, follow me through. Now, starting our descent, set 15″ on the live engine and trim for our downwind speed, 120 Kts. Anticipating 1000′, select 20″, level off and trim for 120 Kts. Don't hesitate to use more power if necessary. It is easy to lose speed on one engine, but difficult to regain it.

We fly crosswind as for a normal circuit, and similarly turn downwind when the tailplane is over the runway. From now on remember that every time you change the power, you also have to adjust the rudder. Monitor the ball and keep it central.

Looking right, all is clear, so turning downwind, aim to roll out with the wingtip running down the runway. Check the speed and the ball. Call:

> Alpha Zulu, downwind asymmetric."
>
> "Alpha Zulu, cleared to finals number one."
>
> "Alpha Zulu.

"Carrying out the downwind checks, avoid lowering the undercarriage too early, but nevertheless don't let this take precedence over the sequence of the drills. Brakes off. Undercarriage down — three greens. Mixture rich. Cowls closed. Induction air cold, check T.'s and P.'s. Propellers fine.

Fuel sufficient and pumps on. Flap — leave up until the base leg. Harness locked. Doors closed.

Now check the speed. We should have at least 100 Kts. before turning base leg. It's getting a bit low, so we must increase power to 24″ to compensate for the drag of the undercarriage. Check the ball and finally trim the rudder; this is the last time we adjust it.

The threshold is 45°, so looking right and left, turn level on to base leg. Rolling out now to allow for the wind, set 14″, lower take-off flap and trim for 100 Kts. We need slight left rudder to centralise the ball. Aim to turn finals at 600′; adjust the power if necessary. Don't forget, every speed or power change will require a rudder input.

Anticipate turning finals to avoid excessive bank. Looking right to check the approach, we can start the turn now, at the same time lowering the nose slightly to maintain 100 Kts. Check undercarriage down, pitch fine and call:

Alpha Zulu, finals asymmetric."

"Alpha Zulu, cleared to land. Wind 270°/10 Kts."

"Alpha Zulu.

Rolling out smoothly, now reduce power slightly to hold 95 Kts., the single-engine climb speed, which we maintain to the critical height, 300′. Remember, we need more throttle than normal to adjust the height and speed. Keep the ball central by co-ordinating rudder movements with the throttle. The approach is standard but don't get too low. Below 300′ or full flap, we are committed to the landing. Leave full flap until we are certain of getting in.

300′ coming up, so progressively reduce the speed to 88 Kts.; avoid raising the nose too much. Now, as we are certain of getting in, lower full flap. Notice I am having to apply right aileron to keep the wings level. Anticipate left rudder when closing the throttle to land.

Flaring now — throttle closed — check the yaw — wings level — hold off — touchdown — gently lower the nose and keep straight with rudder, braking if necessary. If everything is under control, use your surplus speed to pull off the runway.

You may have noticed I closed the zero thrust throttle after touchdown. Remember to do this when flying solo."

END OF EXERCISE.

EXERCISE 23 — MULTI-ENGINE — ASYMMETRIC OVERSHOOT

Aircraft Position in Flight Profile

Aircraft is on an asymmetric final approach, with the left engine at zero thrust, take-off flap and undercarriage down.

Air Exercise

"I have control, follow me through. I will now demonstrate a single-engine overshoot at 400'. Remember the significance of the decision height. At 300' or below, or at any time that we have selected full flap, we are committed to land.

Holding 95 Kts., the single-engine climb speed, we will anticipate 400' slightly to allow for the inertia of the aircraft. 450' coming up, so full power on the right engine, right rudder to balance and smoothly rotate into a shallow climb. Now undercarriage and flaps up to remove the drag, check the ball is central and hold 95 Kts. Trim out the elevator and rudder loads. Call:

> Springfield, Alpha Zulu overshooting."
> "Alpha Zulu."

"Now that we are established in the climb we can turn right to get on the 'dead' side.

The important things to remember when overshooting on one engine, are to be above your safety speed, positively check the yaw with rudder, and raise the undercarriage and flap as soon as possible.

Now you continue with the climb and carry out a circuit and overshoot on one. You have control."

STUDENT PRACTISES.

END OF EXERCISE.

EXERCISE 23 — MULTI-ENGINE — SYNCHRONISING THE ENGINES.

Aircraft Position in Flight Profile

Aircraft climbing after take-off. The student has control.

Air Exercise

"Can your hear the uneven beat of the engines?"

STUDENT ANSWERS

"Clearly, to fly any distance with such a pulsating beat would be tiring and very irritating for you and the passengers. To rectify this, we must synchronise the engines. I have control.

First, set the throttles like this, so that the manifold pressures are exactly the same for both engines. Now adjust the pitch levers to give exactly the same reading on the RPM gauge. If there is still a residual beat, as now, select one of the pitch levers and move it slightly backward or forward. I will move the left one forward, like this. Can you hear that the beat has got worse?"

STUDENT ANSWERS

"Clearly I must move it the other way. You can now hear the beat has improved, and if we make fine adjustments it goes altogether. The engines are now synchronised.

Finally, take note of the exact readings on the RPM gauge, so that, with this aircraft, you will be able to set it precisely first time. I will now upset the power, and I want you to synchronise the engines. You have control."

STUDENT PRACTISES.

END OF EXERCISE.

EXERCISE 23 — MULTI-ENGINE — ENGINE FAILURE AFTER TAKE-OFF

NOTES: (1) When the student practises, it is essential for the instructor to anticipate the yaw before simulating an engine failure.

(2) It is recommended that the throttle is closed smoothly to prevent unbalancing the counter-weights.

Aircraft Position in Flight Profile

Aircraft at the take-off point with checks completed.

Air Exercise

"I want you to carry out a normal take-off, and at 200', I will take over and demonstrate an engine failure after take-off. I will ask you to close the throttle on me and then watch carefully. You have control."

STUDENT PRACTISES.

"I have control. Speed 95 Kts., the single-engine climb speed. Now smoothly close a throttle on me and watch — recovery; check the yaw with rudder — lower the nose here, full power — ball in the centre — check above safety speed, 82 Kts. — dead leg, dead engine — right leg dead, therefore right engine failed — feather starboard, check for fire, work by numbers — touch drills; right mixture idle cut-off — right pitch to feather — right throttle closed — check flap-up safety speed, 88 Kts. — retract the flaps — recheck the ball is central — trim. You have control. Now continue the climb and carry out the checks to secure the engine."

STUDENT PRACTISES.

END OF EXERCISE.

ADVANCED SECTION

ADVANCED ILS.

Aircraft Position in Flight Profile

The PR twin has just intercepted the localiser on a heading of 240°, inbound, in level flight, with the undercarriage down, T/O flap, 100 Kts. and 22″ MP.

Air Exercise

"I have control. I will now demonstrate an alternative method of carrying out an ILS approach, in particular how to hold the glidepath with pitch adjustments. It is sometimes called energy management.

Approaching the outer marker and holding the localiser on a heading of 240°, we should shortly be intercepting the glidepath. We know from experience that to hold the glidepath in this configuration at 100 Kts., we need 14″ manifold pressure with the aeroplane symbol lying on the bottom edge of the horizon. Here comes the ILS glidepath, so anticipating slightly, throttle back to 14″ and select the attitude on the horizon. Wait for the aircraft to settle down and maintain the ILS heading of 240° on the DI. From now on, use the pitch to adjust the glidepath and the power to hold the speed, although to begin with, when the ILS is less sensitive, you will probably have time to co-ordinate both controls. The speed has now settled, but is slightly high at 108 Kts., so throttle back a fraction and raise the nose very slightly; remember the trim change with power.

Although the ILS is still somewhat insensitive at this range, it is obvious that we are going high; there must be very little wind, so lower the aeroplane symbol half a bar width, hold, and trim. Because of the aircraft's inertia with flap and undercarriage down, small pitch adjustments do not immediately result in speed deviations. We will use this to our advantage when the workload is high, but at this range we can ease back the throttle slightly.

As we descend, the ILS becomes more sensitive, and therefore our scan will have to be rapid and selective. The

289

primary performance scan, therefore, should be confined to the ILS and the DI. The secondary scan is the ASI, altimeter and manifold pressure.

The localiser is going left; we must alter course left to make an interception, say 230°. Across to the horizon and apply 10° of bank; pitch is correct. Now roll out on 230°. The localiser is coming in but the glidepath is going up. Back to the horizon and raise the aeroplane symbol a fraction to lie just below the horizon, hold it and trim. Back to the ILS, the localiser is now central again. To hold it we must alter course right to a new heading, let us say 235°. The glidepath is also now central. To hold it, we must lower the pitch and trim.

Remember the fundamental ILS technique. Whenever you regain the glidepath or localiser, you must make a further rate of descent, or heading change, to hold the needles central.

Our scan now, momentarily, includes the altimeter and ASI. The altimeter is reading 800'; about one minute to go before break-off. The ASI is slightly high at 106 Kts., so a fraction back on the power, by a note or two, but hold the attitude against the change of pitch, and retrim. Attitude adjustment for a 5 Kt. correction, is virtually undetectable. Concentrate the scan on the ILS, artificial horizon and the DI. We're going high, so lower the attitude, hold and trim. We're also drifting left, therefore 10° of right bank to check it, but the DI shows we have wandered off heading; let us make the new course 240°. The glidepath is zero again, so lower the symbol to hold; remember the attitude, slightly below the bar. The glidepath is good and the localiser is now central, therefore left on to 235° again. We're going low, so raise the pitch half a bar. Check the altimeter out of the corner of your eye — 200' to go. Now just scan two instruments; the ILS and the horizon, with an occasional glance at the altimeter. 150' to go. Back to the ILS, we're going right and high, therefore lower the pitch and apply left bank, pause, level the wings. Needles within limits and coming in — needles now central, so raise the pitch attitude slightly and apply right bank, pause, level the wings. Altimeter, 30' to go. Now concentrate on the artificial horizon and DI; the mean heading is 235°. Overshooting; full power, aeroplane symbol 2 bar widths high, wings level and right rudder to check the yaw. Now raise the undercarriage and flap, check we are

climbing on the altimeter and call:
Alpha Zulu, overshooting."
"Alpha Zulu, you are cleared to the hold at 2000'."
"Alpha Zulu.
Holding the pitch attitude, check the DI; we have drifted onto 240°, so left bank to regain 235°. Speed 97 Kts., so a fraction lower on the pitch attitude. Now set the QNH on the altimeter and we have completed the overshoot. Continue the climb to 2000' to join the hold for a further ILS. You have control."

STUDENT PRACTISES.

END OF EXERCISE.

ADVANCED SECTION

ADVANCED SHORT-FIELD LANDING

Aircraft Position in Flight Profile

Aircraft turning on to base leg.

Air Exercise

"I have control. I will now show you an approach and short-field landing, with an alternative method of controlling the speed and the glidepath, and a more sophisticated technique for ensuring an exact touchdown point.

As usual on base leg, lower half flap and trim for 80 Kts. Aim to turn finals slightly lower than usual, say 400', so that we have a lower approach path to cross the airfield boundary at about 10 — 15', to land as near to the fence as reasonably safe. Looking left to clear the approach, turn now, still maintaining 80 Kts. Call:

> Alpha Zulu, finals."
> "Alpha Zulu, you are cleared to land. Wind 260/10 Kts."
> "Alpha Zulu.

Rolling out now, immediately lower full flap and reduce the speed to 75 Kts. as standard. Our glidepath is critical, so for both speed and glidepath corrections, use the throttle as the lead control; only making small pitch adjustments for speed and rather more for the glidepath. Remember to hold the pitch attitude whenever you feel a trim change with power.

Our glidepath is good but our speed is 80 Kts., 5 Kts. too high. Reduce the power a note or two, approximately 50 RPM, and retrim. Now with about 500 yards to go, select 60 Kts., the threshold speed, by reducing the power slightly and raising the nose a fraction — 60 Kts., so increase the power slightly to hold the speed and trim the attitude. From here on 'bracket' the speed with small power adjustments, but you must hold the pitch steady. Aim the glidepath at the touchdown point with the elevators, always matching pitch changes with power to peg the speed; nose-up more power, nose-down less power. Now as the nose comes abeam the boundary, concentrate on the flightpath, the boundary and touchdown point. You must have power on at the flare; reapply if necessary. Flaring now, pause, power off — minimum hold-off — touch down — lower the nose — maximum braking, stick back, check power off, and keep straight with rudder.

The most likely causes of an undershoot when the glidepath is critical, are using the elevator as the sole means of speed control, and looking at the airspeed indicator when close to the boundary. The secret is to stabilise the aircraft at the threshold speed well short of the boundary. You can always practise precision airspeed and glidepath control, at high altitude."

END OF EXERCISE.

ADVANCED SECTION
EXERCISE 15 — MAXIMUM POSSIBLE RATE TURNS

NOTE: (1) This exercise requires prudence and instructors must stress that it should only be flown in aeroplanes certificated for aerobatics and fitted with an accelerometer.

Aircraft Position in Flight Profile

Aircraft at 3000'. HASELL checks complete.

Air Exercise

"You saw in the max. rate level turn how, even with full power set, the speed decreased quickly to about 70 Kts. and we were only pulling $2\frac{1}{2}$ 'G'. Remember the 4 maximums you need for a maximum possible rate turn: maximum speed, maximum power, maximum 'G' and maximum CL, that is on the buffet burble, For this exercise we'll take the maximum permitted 'G' as 4, to avoid overstressing the aircraft and so that we don't tire ourselves too much. Remember to tense your stomach muscles before the 'G' comes on.

Let's have a look at a turn to the right, follow me through. A good lookout all round and roll into the turn. Applying full power, ease on to the 'burble'. Now, before the speed stabilises at 70 Kts., overbank to let the nose drop below the horizon. The speed is increasing steadily, but keep the pull on to hold the burble. You can also feel the 'G' building up, so tense your tummy but still maintain the pull. 130 Kts. coming up, so reduce the bank slightly and hold the picture. We are indicating 4G, 130 Kts., full power and we're on the burble. This is the maximum possible rate turn with our limit of 4G, but you can see we're losing height rapidly. Rolling out, we will level off and relax.

You can see that it's quite a strain even at 4G. When you have mastered the technique and can quickly enter a maximum possible rate turn at 4G, we'll have a look at one at the aircraft's 'G' limit.

Try a turn yourself to the right and then practise a few more turns alternating left and right. You have control."

STUDENT PRACTISES.
END OF EXERCISE.

ADVANCED SECTION
FIXED-POINT NAVIGATION
Aircraft Position in Flight Profile

Aircraft approaching the starting point at 2000' and 90 Kts., the cruise speed.

Air Exercise

"You can see the start point, the airfield at 12 o'clock, range about 3 miles. We have approximately 2 minutes before we are overhead, so let us check the map. The heading required is 315°, at 2000' and the stopwatch is zero. As we are well within 45° of the track heading, we can hold 350° until almost overhead, before turning.

Now crossing the airfield boundary, turn left on to 315° and start the watch. Recheck our heading and finally confirm that the watch is actually running.

Read the map by holding it level with the coaming, so that we can also maintain our lookout. We have made no allowance for wind and can therefore expect to pick up drift, which we will assess at our first checkpoint. You can see on the map that we should fly over a road just to the left of a small town at 4 minutes. In the meantime, hold an exact heading which is fundamental to fixed-point navigation.

2 minutes to the feature, so look ahead about 3 miles. You can see the town and road. It is obvious that we are going to pass over the town itself, so we have a crosswind from the left. Using the drift line, I estimate that we are about 3° off track. Now, unlike normal pilot navigation, we 'dog-leg' visually back onto track again. In this case, we aim the aircraft just to the left of the town. Once we are back on track, we will take up our heading again, plus or minus the drift, in this case 312°.

Now, alongside the town, turn right on to 312° and check the stopwatch — it is 4 minutes; we are on time. As our next 'fix' is at 10 minutes on the stopwatch, we can put the map away until we are within two minutes of it, or until 8 minutes is up.

8 minutes on the stopwatch, so map up to see the next fix. We fly just to the right of a small lake in some woods, and then directly over a small town, which sits on a railway line at right angles to our track.

There are the woods and the lake and, looking ahead, I can see the town at 12 o'clock, so it seems that our wind correction is good. All we need to do is to check our ETA at the 10 minute mark — about 30 seconds beyond the town.

Crossing the railway line now, wait for 30 seconds to check the time — 11 minutes, we are 1 minute late. As we are about halfway, our ETA at Cheddar will be 2 minutes late or 23 minutes on the stopwatch. We are on track, we have established our drift and revised our ETA. All we have to do now is to steer an exact heading, maintain our speed and rely on the stopwatch.

You can fly it from here to the next turning point. Use the map allied with the time to identify the next fix feature and the turning point. You will have ample time for a LIFE check, after you have settled down. Tell me when you see the town. You have control."

STUDENT PRACTISES.

"I have control. Yes, that is correct, and the turning point is that small lake beyond the town. We have checked the DI against the compass, and the new heading is 184° for 15 minutes without any correction for wind. However, we know from the last leg that the wind must be roughly Westerly to North-Westerly, and probably about 10 Kts. Normally we would allow for this on the next leg, but on this occasion I won't so that I can demonstrate a further aspect of fixed-point navigation.

Now over the lake, look out — turn left and stop the watch; the time is 22½ minutes; our revised ETA was quite accurate. Rolling out on heading restart the watch, and as usual we must check H — heading 184°, A — altitude 2000′ and T — time, the watch is running.

Looking at the map, our initial check heading is that we pass about 1 mile to the right of a small town. The first fix is when we cross a disused railway line at 4 minutes, about 1 mile left of a junction and on the Westerly edge of a wood.

Look ahead and you can see that we will pass fairly close to the small town; we are drifting left as we would expect with this wind. We will wait until the fix, in 4 minutes, to make a heading alteration. This time we will use a DR heading change to regain track. For fixed-point navigation we make a standard alteration of 30° and, for 90 Kts., hold it for 1 minute 20 seconds for every mile off track. We then turn on to heading again plus or minus the drift.

Can you see the old railway track and woods ahead?"

STUDENT ANSWERS

"Good, the planned track goes down the West side of the wood, but you can see we are to the left, about 1 mile off track. The drift therefore, since the turning point, is 1 mile in 6, or 10° by the 1 in 60 rule.

Over the railway line now, turn right 30° onto 214° and check the time — 4 minutes. Our ETA at our next turning point should be correct, but, to get back on track we must hold this heading for 1 minute 20 seconds, or until 5 minutes 20 seconds on the stopwatch. In the meantime we can calculate our new heading when we have regained track. We must allow 10° for drift, so our heading will have to be 194°.

5 minutes 20 seconds on the stopwatch, so turn left onto 194°. Now that we are back on track again concentrate on steering a precise heading and holding 90 Kts.

We use this technique for track correction, if the ground beyond the fix is featureless; it can be quite useful on occasions.

Now you continue with the exercise. Remember, fixed point navigation is a combination of track crawling, selective map reading related to the stopwatch, and above all accurate course keeping. it is a systematic technique to mitigate 'brain failure'. You have control."

STUDENT PRACTISES.

END OF EXERCISE.